Engraving and Decorating
GLASS

Engraving
and
Decorating
Glass

Barbara Norman

McGraw-Hill Book Company
New York : St. Louis : San Francisco

To my Mother

First published in the United States by McGraw-Hill Book Company, a subsidiary of McGraw-Hill, Inc., 1972.

SBN: 07-047215-7

Library of Congress Catalog Card Number: 72-1989

First Edition

Set in Bembo by C. E. Dawkins (Typesetters) Ltd., S.E.1 and printed by Lowe & Brydone (Printers) Ltd., in Great Britain for David & Charles (Publishers) Limited South Devon House Newton Abbot Devon

Contents

List of Plates

B

Photographs not acknowledged above are from the author's collection.

Foreword

My first acquaintance with the work of Barbara Norman sprang from our mutual involvement in a world far removed from the delicate art of decorating glass. It was in Broadcasting House, in London, that I found myself engaged in one of those casually friendly conversations that gather momentum from one meeting to the next and eventually lead to something quite unexpected.

One of the pleasures of working in a large organisation is the wealth and variety of talents that flower privately in one's colleagues. You quickly learn not to stereotype people in crude terms of the job they do. Once off duty they may shine with an unsuspected lustre as falconers or campanologists or designers of model aircraft. Even so, Barbara Norman surprised me when, in the course of some talk between us about the pleasures of handling good glass, she let fall the fact that her hours of leisure were preoccupied with the difficulties of engraving glass. After all, how many people engrave glass in their spare time?

The day came when I was privileged to see some of her work. At that time I believe she had confined her designs to floral subjects and I suppose it was inevitable that, as a notorious ornithological bore, I should seek to interest her in birds as models. My first suggestions, mainly photographs of birds, were technically unsuitable so I recommended the classic engravings of Thomas Bewick as subjects with interesting possibilities in the medium of glass. And I asked Barbara if she would accept a commission from me to make a set of wineglasses engraved with subjects drawn from Bewick's work—one of them, since I like puns, to be a hawk. She took me up on that, and in due course I became the proud owner of a fine set of bird-embellished glasses.

Like all patrons, from the Medici downwards, I was pleased to have my discernment confirmed by public opinion. Miss Norman's work began to attract attention outside her circle of friends and she was invited to put her work on display in exhibitions of contemporary craftsmanship. In recent years she has exhibited regularly at the Royal Society of Miniature Painters, Engravers and Sculptors; the United Society of Artists; and the Society of Women Artists, of which she has been elected a member. I believe she has the rigorous and determined self-criticism which eventually separates the professional from the gifted amateur. She has certainly pushed herself a long way without much encouragement, because when I asked her how she started to learn this unusual art she told me that she had perforce to teach herself. She had no teacher and she could find no book that showed a beginner the elementary mistakes to avoid, the tools to buy, the glass to select.

'Is there no book at all on the subject?' I asked.

'None that I can find.'

'Then why not write one yourself?'

Happily she did. This is it.

Desmond Hawkins

Introduction

The purpose of this book is to offer what I hope will be new fields of interest for those who want to do creative work of some kind, but who have not been able to discover the right medium. I myself had been interested in drawing and painting, but there came a moment when I realised that I wanted some kind of work which would involve a craft as well as art. For me, the answer to this proved to be diamond point engraving on glass; so I set out to discover more about it.

To my surprise this proved to be very difficult. My mind was full of questions about the methods of work, the tools one would need, the glass itself, but finding the answers was a difficult matter. It soon became clear to me that little guidance was available for beginners, and that many established engravers were self-taught; the only way was just to launch out on the work for oneself. I have therefore written this book as a result of what I discovered by means of work and research, and as a result of much helpful talk with others, especially with Mary Stephens and students at Morley College, London.

My enjoyment of diamond point engraving led to a wider interest in many other aspects of glass decorating, and of using glass itself as a decoration as in mosaics and panelling. I realised that here was a material which offered a wide field of pleasurable work, ranging from the seriously professional to the enjoyably amateur. Almost every method of working with glass has its roots deep in the past, so in discussing the possible methods of work I have sometimes written briefly of what has been achieved in earlier times. Many techniques may be used, unchanged, to day; some may be adapted with the help of modern materials. Most of the work described can be done without the need of a studio or workshop, and most of the materials are reasonably priced.

As an appreciation and understanding of one's materials always adds greatly to the interest and enjoyment of any work, I have begun with short chapters on the development of glass itself, and on the way in which it is made.

CHAPTER 1

The Development of Glass

Many people think of glass—if they think about it at all—in very general terms. They are aware that it can be blown in some way, that there are such things as stained glass, cut glass and Venetian glass, that it is sometimes engraved, and that nowadays much of it comes from Czechoslovakia and Sweden. All these generalisations are true, but behind the bare facts lies a long and fascinating history much of which is bound up with decoration of one kind or another since, right from its beginnings, glass was a luxury article and much creative effort was lavished on it. Only relatively recently, with the introduction of mass production, has it been thought of by so many people as a very ordinary, everyday product.

EARLIEST GLASS

How it all started is not known for certain, but an accidental discovery is accepted as at least likely. A story told by Pliny is generally not now believed, though no better explanation has been forthcoming so far. According to Pliny, some merchants sailing in the Mediterranean camped ashore for the night on the estuary of the river Belus. They made a fire for cooking, and supported their cooking pots on some of the blocks of natron (a form of soda) which they were carrying as cargo. Later, they discovered that the heat of the fire had fused the natron and sand into a substance which was new to them—glass. And ever since those remote times, soda and silica have formed the basis of glass, although as time went by and knowledge and skill increased, other ingredients were added to produce stability and strength, or colour, or clarity. Pliny wrote in the first century AD, but the earliest piece of glass ever found is a bead discovered in Egypt, and which has been dated at about 3000 BC. There is thus a very large gap in time between Pliny's story and the probable first use of glass so the facts may never now be known.

At first, glass was not blown at all. That process came much later. The Egyptians had some very early uses of glass, putting it on pottery as a glaze. Then came glass objects, such as the bead already mentioned and finally glass shapes which could support themselves. These early glass vessels were made by a most ingenious process called core-winding. A central shape or core was made of some material, possibly clay bound with straw. A rod was attached to this core, and threads of molten glass were trailed over the core until it was completely covered, the whole being frequently reheated to keep it in a workable condition. One of the earliest known glass vessels made by this method is a small vase owned by the British Museum, dated at some time between 2050 and 2000 BC. Beautiful and complicated decorations were often applied, including the fixing of handles and the trailing of threads of glass over the main part of the vessel; some sort of comb-like tool was used to make them into patterns of wavy lines. This kind of decoration, although extremely simple, is very attractive: it reminds me irresistibly of the icing on French mille-feuilles pastries—where indeed pretty much the same method is used to get the wavy lines! In due course the glass was cooled, the rod removed and the core scraped out.

The whole method sounds primitive, but vessels of great beauty were made in this way. Enormous care was taken to remove any defects which—inevitably—appeared, and the cooled glass was ground and polished. If the opening in the neck of the vessel was large enough, as much as possible of the inside was smoothed out too. When it is remembered what a difficult substance glass is to work on compared with, for example, clay, these early glass vessels are amazingly well made. One can only marvel at the way a molten substance which can never even be touched—let alone molded—by hand is shaped into such graceful objects.

Glassmaking gradually took root not only in Egypt, where Alexandria was a great manufacturing centre for many centuries, but in other areas of the Middle East, particularly Syria. Throughout the following centuries, both Alexandrian and Syrian glassmaking reached very high standards. The two styles developed separately, Syrian glass becoming more ornate than Alexandrian.

The development of glass followed a very leisurely course: not until somewhere around 50 BC, several thousand years after its unknown beginning, a further discovery was made that molten glass could be blown into shapes on the end of a hollow rod. As in the discovery of making glass, the origins of blowing it are unknown. It is most likely to have been an accidental discovery, but however it came about it was a development of tremendous importance and, apart from various refinements introduced down the centuries, the actual technique of blowing glass, and the tools used, have ever since remained basically the same. Today, when nothing seems to last for five minutes without change and upheaval, and where planned obsolescence is part of life, this thousands of years old continuity of glassmaking methods is a most satisfying thought.

ROMAN GLASS

Spreading round the Mediterranean area, glassmaking was practised in turn by the Greeks and the Romans. Roman glass denotes glass of that period rather than glass made by the citizens of Rome themselves, as Rome was not an important centre of manufacture. The Romans appear to have known just about everything as far as glass is concerned except how to make pure sparkling crystal: the world had to wait many centuries for that. The discovery of blowing glass quickly resulted in a great freedom for craftsmen, and Roman glassmakers developed all kinds of techniques. They knew how to engrave it, both in the manner of engravers of precious stones, and in the cameo technique, and also used some kind of sharp tool to produce what was to be the forerunner of diamond point engraving. They could enamel it, gild it, and even use engraved gold sandwiched between two layers of glass—a means of decoration successfully used again in Germany and Bohemia, long after in the eighteenth century. Their glass was often made in a variety of colours, some of which were due to impurities which at that time it was beyond anyone's knowledge to remove. This was particularly true of the greens which began to predominate. As well as making glass by the blowing method, the Romans continued to use molds for some kind of work, particularly when making plaques with any kind of molded design upon them.

The Romans also did some very beautiful work by means of fused glass mosaics. This is just another example of their skill because today, nearly 2,000 years later, people are again doing much the same kind of work with every modern aid, including small electric kilns. Roman fused glass mosaics were made by arranging pieces of different coloured glass in haphazard patterns and fusing them in a furnace. Plaques made by this method were used as jewellery or were inlaid in furniture. Mosaic patterned glass bowls were also made by reheating pieces of coloured glass in a mold. These were known as murrhine bowls.

Roman glass was usually useful, generally decorative, and always extremely elegant. Much of it now has an attractive iridescence as a result of the physical conditions in which it has remained through many centuries; if it has spent hundreds of years buried in dampness it often has an attractive pearly gleam. Many hundreds of years later, towards the end of the nineteenth century, an American, Tiffany, made extensive research into Roman methods of manufacture in an effort to reproduce the iridescence of so much Roman glass. He succeeded in producing what became known as Favrile glass.

The 400 years approximately of the Roman Empire provided the most civilised, well governed and settled conditions the Western world had ever known, and during that time the art of making glass spread to all parts of her vast territory. Glassmakers were often wanderers by temperament, especially the Syrians and, as a result of this, glasshouses were set up further and further afield, spreading gradually northwards over Europe. Apart from an individual's personal desire for change, there was often a real need to move in order to ensure a supply of raw materials. Glasshouses used a vast amount of wood for fuel, as well as quantities of sand: as an illustration of the amount of wood used, glassmakers in England in 1615 were forbidden to use it for fuel because they had made such inroads into the forests. The centres of glassmaking changed constantly over the centuries. In the West, the Roman Empire was already in decay by the beginning of the sixth century and in the resulting chaos all artistic endeavour suffered greatly. But eastwards, in Byzantium and the Near East, this was a time of expansion.

VENETIAN AND GERMAN GLASS

In Western Europe the Dark Ages closed in, and what remained of glassmaking had to be adapted to changed conditions and to fight for survival. Glasshouses, however, appeared towards the north in an area bounded by the Seine and Rhine, and a distinctive kind of Forest glass, called Waldglas, was developed from local ingredients, the alkali content of the glass being obtained from wood ash from the abundant forests. This resulted in a natural colouring of varying pale greens and ambers. The elaborate and beautiful decorations of the Roman world disappeared and there was no more painting, gilding or cutting. However, a modest kind of trail decoration continued to be used. Unlike the north, Venice did not suffer nearly so much during the Dark Ages. By the time of the Crusades, Venetian glass was already highly developed and the commercially minded Venetians were trading far afield.

Ever since the beginning of glassmaking, craftsmen had been striving to make a clear glass, as nearly as possible like natural rock crystal. This goal had often been set aside in the interest of making glass of varied colours, but basically it was always there. At last, in the fifteenth century, the Venetians produced a clear, delicate glass which they called 'cristallo'. In a thick state this was not entirely clear, having a slight greyness, but if blown very thin the greyness almost disappeared: thus began the very distinctive glass whose delicate appearance has come to be linked in most people's minds with Venice. This fine glass was too thin and brittle for cutting or wheel engraving. A limited amount of diamond point engraving was used on it, but it was not generally very suitable for any kind of surface cutting and, because of its fragile nature, decoration was added at the time of manufacture. This added decoration became more and more elaborate and complicated with a great deal of frothy-looking exterior decoration, and almost any very elaborate glass came to mean 'Venetian glass' to future generations.

The Venetians learned how to manipulate glass as no one had done before. Being near the sea, their alkali came from seaweed ash. Glass made of this could be kept in a workable state over a wide range of temperatures, which is one reason why Venetian glass was fashioned into such elaborate patterns.

The Venetians recognised the value of the industry and grouped all glassmakers on the island of Murano, forbidding them to divulge their methods of work or to leave Venice to work elsewhere. However, a famous glassmaking industry was also developing in Altare, near Genoa, and some Venetians did manage to leave Murano to join the Altare craftsmen. In that way, Venetian methods of glassmaking, and Venetian styles, very gradually spread further and further northwards because the Altare industry was not subject to controls and its craftsmen had complete freedom to move as they wished.

The Venetians loved to decorate. They coloured their glass, combining several colours in one object. They painted it in all kinds of ways, sometimes using enamels on clear glass, sometimes painting landscapes on opaque white glass, as for example the eighteenth-century Venetian scenes after Canaletto. They gilded too. But one of the most beautiful and complicated forms of decoration which they invented was 'latticinio'. This was achieved by putting threads of opaque white glass inside clear glass so that when the glass was blown and fashioned in a particular way, the opaque threads arranged themselves into elaborate, perfectly accurate patterns spiralling round the glass or criss-crossing through it. It is elegant and controlled, rather like some kind of interior engraving.

It always seems to me that the Venetians must have greatly enjoyed their glassmaking because their work radiates confidence and pleasure. They appear to have flung themselves wholeheartedly into an absolute welter of inventive shapes and decorations, and only very occasionally to have overdone it a little. It is difficult to imagine their agonising over their work. It seems far more likely that they tossed it off with cheerful pleasure, loving the colours and patterns. Nowadays we can appreciate the natural colours and comfortable shapes of the northern Waldglas, but to people living at the time the clear, fragile Venetian glass must have seemed highly desirable and very civilised. It was a great luxury, which is hardly surprising when one considers the tremendous difficulty of transporting such fragile objects by the means then available. How much must have been broken as it bumped over the rough unsurfaced roads.

Much admired though Venetian glass was, distinctive styles of material and design were developing in other parts of Europe, for instance the use of glass as a decorative material in stained glass windows. Coloured glass windows were known in Europe by the ninth century, and by the thirteenth century this form of decorative glass had reached its greatest heights. There still remains a great deal to be seen throughout Europe, ranging from a single window in many small country churches to the magnificence of great cathedral windows.

By the middle of the sixteenth century, the Germans were producing tall, sturdy cylindrical glasses, known as Humpen. These were made of Waldglas and came to be lavishly decorated with enamel. All kinds of subjects were used—coats of arms, scenes from daily life, working themes connected with various guilds. Like the Venetians, the Germans were great decorators of glass, but the two styles were very different. In contrast to the delicate, artificially coloured, elaborate Venetian glass, German glass was mostly the fairly thick Waldglas, with a natural colouring of green or amber. So the Germans concentrated on painted decoration and on the developing art of wheel engraving, rather than on elaborations of the glass itself. They also developed a method of making a rich ruby-red glass, using minute particles of pure gold.

In Bohemia, thicker glass was made and this went well with wheel engraving which demanded something substantial for the wheel to cut into. Bohemian glass has always held a high position and during the Baroque period, when the popularity of Venetian glass had declined, Bohemia became a world centre for the manufacture of luxury glass. All kinds of decoration were used, but wheel engraving achieved the greatest fame.

DUTCH GLASS

The Netherlands became a meeting point for the various existing styles of glass. Much was imported from Venice, and from the northern centres of Waldglas which were near at hand. Their own manufacture was centred on Liège and Antwerp, and the Dutch particularly developed the style of the Römer, a drinking glass also popular in Germany. These glasses can often be seen in the detailed Dutch paintings of the seventeenth century. But gradually the Dutch turned more to decorating imported glass than to making their own, and they developed this art to a very high level. They engraved both by the copper wheel method and by diamond point. Their superb hand engraving was, and still is, without equal.

FRENCH GLASS

France is particularly noted for three kinds of glass development. In the Middle Ages, French stained glass windows were at their height as in the cathedrals of Chartres and Poitiers; in the seventeenth century the French not only started making mirrors but broke the monopoly of the Venetians; and towards the end of the same century they invented the first process of making plate glass. The manufacture of table glass tended to lag behind but this was offset to some extent by the establishment of the famous factory at Baccarat in 1765. This became particularly well known for the production of millefiore paperweights. France has never been a centre of applied decoration, but in modern times—from the nineteenth century onwards—much attention has been paid to design. Names to note among modern manufacturers are Lalique and Daum.

ENGLISH GLASS

In England, glassmaking had a chequered history. During the Dark Ages, as in so many other areas in Europe, there had been very little activity: there was not much place for such a fragile luxury as glass in the uncertain and dangerous everyday life of those unsettled centuries. Around the early thirteenth century, however, when conditions were far better, glass-making began to revive, the centre of activity being a small hamlet in the thickly wooded Weald area of Surrey, near Chiddingfold. The Weald in

Wineglass with diamond point engraving. English, dated 1581, and probably made in the glasshouse of Giacomo Verzelini in London

C

general was an iron producing area, but in the mid-thirteenth century an immigrant Frenchman from Normandy, Laurence Vitrearius, established himself there and became renowned for church windows, receiving orders for no less a building than Westminster Abbey and, later, for St George's Chapel, Windsor. He was followed in the same locality by two other families, one also of Norman origin, and between them they made glass in that area for over 300 years. Other glass centres existed throughout the Weald, its abundant wood fuel serving the glassmakers as it had for centuries served the ancient ironworks. Natural green-coloured Wealden glass, much like Waldglas, was produced in some quantity and acquired a considerable reputation in England.

So glassmaking in England pursued its leisurely course until the arrival in the late sixteenth century of a Lorrainer, Jean Carré, who had learned his craft in the great glassmaking centre of Antwerp and was familiar with Venetian methods and styles. Hitherto, Venetian glass had been a great luxury in England, imported with much difficulty across a considerable distance. Carré was followed by other continental glassmakers among whom was Verzelini, a Venetian, who was to rise to much fame. When Carré died, Verzelini took over his glassworks and manufactured glass in the Venetian style (see also p. 51).

Yet, all the time, the search was continually going on for clear crystal glass. At last, in the late 1600s, the answer was found by George Ravenscroft with an invention which represented the greatest development in glassmaking for many centuries and which was to have an enormous effect on glassmaking throughout the world. He finally perfected the process of making glass with flint as one of the ingredients and produced a truly clear, sparkling glass. This was not achieved without many setbacks while the exact proportions of flint were being worked out, and Ravenscroft's early attempts were liable to break down into multitudes of tiny cracks known as 'crizzling'. However, eventually he righted these defects by using lead oxide, and by 1675 lead crystal glass was here for good. This clear glass represented a tremendous advance. When unadorned, it had a clarity hitherto unknown. For purposes of all kinds of engraving it was very much softer and more responsive than the harder, more brittle soda glass. It could be made to any chosen thickness and still retain its brilliance, so it was just as suitable for copper wheel engrav-

Wineglass, probably
English, with dia-
mond point stipple
engraving, by David
Wolff, c 1786

ing or for cutting as it was for the very delicate diamond point method.

The next century was the best age of English glass, not only in the field of design but also in the methods of decoration used—coloured glass, engraving, enamelling, cutting. The name most associated with the enamelled decoration of that period is that of William Beilby. His was a family full of talent: William and his sister Mary were both skilled enamellers, the sister probably helping the brother with his work. Unfortunately Mary fell ill while still in her early twenties and was unable to continue her painting. William is famous for his heraldic work, but after some years he extended his range of subjects to include landscapes. Ralph, another brother, was also a glass enameller, and between them they decorated glasses with pastoral or sporting scenes, birds, classical buildings, as well as more conventional designs like barley or vines. However, they are probably best known for their magnificent, coloured heraldic designs.

In the eighteenth century, too, another kind of painted decoration on glass was extremely popular. This was the work of Michael Edkins, who worked on pure white opaque glass made in Bristol. This was intentionally made to look like porcelain, and Edkins' paintings make the similarity even more marked. Bristol was also famous for a deep blue glass, gilded with rather conventional designs; the gold on blue produced an extremely rich effect.

SCANDINAVIAN GLASS

Nowadays, Scandinavia occupies a prominent position in the manufacture of glass. Her fame rests more upon present-day ouput than on past achievements and her reputation rests almost exclusively on an elegant purity of line with no added decoration and on a concentration on the functional.

AMERICAN GLASS

America inevitably came upon the scene at a fairly late stage in the history of glass development, when most technical problems had been solved. The early days of the industry were difficult, and one after another the glassmaking ventures faded out. The first American glasshouse was established at Jamestown in 1608, and great names of the past are Caspar Wistar, William Henry Stiegel and John Frederick Amelung, who all worked during the eighteenth century. Their surviving glasses are now prized by collectors.

In the last ten years or so of the last century and roughly the first fifteen years of the present century, the work of an American artist, Louis Comfort Tiffany, made a considerable impact on the world of glass making. Tiffany, who was born in 1848 and died in 1933, was a man of extremely varied artistic interests and talents. He first won recognition as a painter, and studied in Paris. By 1879 his interests had centred upon interior decorating and in the course of this he began to concentrate upon glass in many forms. He became particularly interested in iridescence in glass, and immersed himself in experimenting with methods of producing this. Eventually Tiffany's iridescent glass, which he called 'Favrile Glass', became world famous. Its development coincided with the art nouveau movement at the turn of the last century, and his glass is an outstanding feature of that movement. Nowadays, any piece of Tiffany glass is either prized by a collector or owned by a museum.

Probably one of America's greatest contributions to the development of glassmaking was the invention of press-molding early in the nineteenth century. Molded glass had been known for many centuries but the Americans were the first to adapt it as a factory-type enterprise. For molding, the designs had to have clear, precise lines and they were incised onto molds which were made up of several pieces. There was not much limitation on what could be made by this process, except that some kinds of broad-rimmed plates were difficult. Molten glass was poured into the mold and a plunger forced the glass into every cavity, at the same time hollowing out the centre. Patterns were extremely beautiful, and often looked like fine lace. As manufacturing methods improved, it became possible to make two or more articles at the same time.

No remarks on developments in American glassmaking would be complete without some reference to what is known all over the world as some of the most beautiful and original glass it is possible to see—Steuben glass. It is identified in most people's minds with its magnificent copper wheel engraved decoration, but for those who look further than exterior embellishment it is at once apparent that the glass itself has a distinctive quality. It is the clearest, most luminous crystal that can be imagined but, perhaps because of the shapes of the finished pieces and the unusual thickness of many of them, it gives a curious effect of arrested movement. It is as if a slow-moving river of molten glass has momentarily paused and, for a brief space of time, formed itself into beautiful shapes before once more flowing onwards. This sense of mobility is, for me at any rate, the particular charm of Steuben glass. Such is the position now attained by this unique glass that there is hardly a state visit, royal wedding or major international occasion which is not marked by a specially created presentation piece.

CHAPTER 2

Methods of Glassmaking

It always adds greatly to the enjoyment of any craft if one has some understanding and appreciation of the material being used. So before starting to describe some of the ways in which glass may be decorated it may be helpful to give a short outline of the way it is made—a fascinating process.

Once the art of blowing glass had been discovered at some period around 50 BC, the tools and methods of the craft hardly changed during something like 1,900 years. The aims of the glassmaker of course differed greatly through the centuries, following fashions in shapes and decorations, but the methods of producing the great variety of styles which flourished at various times remained unaltered.

In some respects, glassmaking is still the same today. The task of the glassmaker is, as it has always been, to transmute an extremely hot molten mass of treacly consistency, which cannot be handled, into the type and shape of glass required, striving always for perfection. The basic ingredients too, remain little changed. Soda glass still consists, with very few variations, of silica sand, soda ash and limestone. Lead crystal, although varied by individual glasshouses to create their own particular type of glass, is still composed of silica sand (with as little iron as possible), potash and lead oxide.

Even present day methods of colouring glass by adding metallic oxides were known and used thousands of years ago. In early times, both cobalt

31

and copper were available, making it possible to produce blue and green glass. The famous ruby-red glass developed at Potsdam around 1680 was made by the addition of gold, and even today glass of this particular rich red colour is still made by adding real gold to the batch. The following table gives an idea of some of the colouring methods used:

Glass	Colouriser
Green	Chromium, iron, copper
Red	Gold, copper, selenium
Yellow	Cadmium, sulphur
Blue	Cobalt, copper
Violet	Manganese
Yellow-green	Chromium oxide and uranium

But although, in these respects, glassmaking is still unaltered, modern methods have revolutionised the old methods of working. Today most glass is entirely machine-made by extremely sophisticated methods of mass production. Containers of all kinds emerge relentlessly from assembly lines; plate glass and sheet glass, plain and coloured, are made on a vast scale by modern processes. Some of this glass reaches a very high standard of quality. Much of it, as we shall see in the next chapter, is suitable for the decorative methods described in this book. The very finest engraving glass however is handmade and, amidst all this welter of mechanisation, craftsmen are still working steadily on, making each individual glass by the unchanging hand-blown process. Both soda glass and lead crystal can be handmade, but it is crystal glass which gives the most beautiful effects.

Handmade glass, either soda glass or lead crystal, is distinguishable by its fine finish from that which is machine-made. However good the latter may be, and some of it is extremely attractive, it never attains the brilliance of hand-blown glass, and in many cases, when glass has been made by machine, it is possible to see the fine joins in the mold.

Since the first step in making glass was to produce a molten mass, the furnace itself was of the greatest importance. Prints of old glasshouses show comparatively small clay furnaces with clay pots above. Small glassmaking concerns had to economise and build three-level furnaces, shaped like beehives. The bottom layer was for the fire, the middle for founding, and the top for annealing. More prosperous glasshouses built two or three furnaces with separate annealing chambers.

Modern glassworks making hand-blown glass still use what seem to be quite small clay pots; in fact, they hold a ton of glass. Many glassworks make their own pots, and this is a highly skilled job. They must be perfect, and are made by hand using only the simplest potters' tools. Unless subjected to special modern drying methods each pot needs many weeks to dry out. Even with modern quick-drying, it is from six to eight weeks before a new pot can be used. When dry, it is fired and carefully tested for cracks. These clay pots are a nightmare for glassmakers. Their average life is only thirteen weeks, and they must constantly be watched for cracks; if a crack is not noticed, a ton of molten glass will pour out and be wasted.

Installing new pots is a very taxing and dangerous job. They are generally grouped together in a circle in the middle of the glasshouse floor, facing outwards from the furnace. The furnace never goes out, and the combined heat from all the pots is tremendous. When a new pot is installed this has to be done in the middle of what must seem like an inferno, while all the other pots continue to be heated to capacity. The new pot, already fired and tested, is heated again so that it is hot during the installation process.

All old illustrations of glassmakers at work show a busy, well populated scene, and this is inevitable as the making of each individual piece of glass is the result of the work of a team of four men. Again, this method of work has not changed over the centuries. The team consists of a master craftsman (the gaffer), a servitor (also a skilled craftsman), a footmaker, and a boy. The footmaker is an apprentice. Since the gaffer does much of his work of modelling (marvering) and blowing while sitting in a chair, the team itself has become known as a 'chair'.

The glassmakers' tools, of ancient design, are made either of iron or wood. Ideally, the wood is pear; failing that, mahogany will do. The reason for this is that the wood must be free from resin, which would ruin the hot glass. These wooden tools gradually char and burn when in contact with the glass, and a soft charcoal surface is formed which is smooth to use on the viscous glass.

Molten glass is made by tipping into the pot furnace all the ingredients at once—very carefully measured. Also included is a specific quantity of broken glass known as cullet. This must be made of glass of exactly the same constituents as the glass which is about to be made, otherwise it will be incompatible and the glass will be spoilt. Cullet is usually made up of the glassworks' own rejects and breakages, and its addition helps the raw materials to melt and fuse more quickly. It is also an economical way of disposing of inevitable breakages. All this is then heated to about 1500° C (2732° F), impurities and gases rising to the top just as with cooking in one's own kitchen. After some thirty-six hours or so, when the glass is completely fluid, it is cooled so that it reaches the consistency of treacle, but is still extremely hot. Work on it can now be started.

The impression given by a modern glassworks is of organised, efficient confusion. No doubt it has always been so. Centrally, there is the main circular furnace with its several individual pots. Chairs (using the word to mean the four-man team) are grouped round it, allowing each an adequate working space. Each chair has a small auxiliary furnace, known as a glory-hole, in which glass is reheated from time to time during the making of a vessel. This keeps it at a workable consistency. The gaffer's tools are grouped round his chair, and the chair itself has broad, slightly sloping arms with an iron surface upon which the glass is rolled or marvered.

The footmaker takes a blowing iron to the furnace and gathers on the end of it a blob of glass of exactly the right size to make the desired vessel. He marvers it on the iron slab by rolling the blowing iron to and fro so that the blob of glass is smoothed into a symmetrical shape. When necessary, the glass is reheated in the glory-hole and it is then blown once or twice until it has formed a small balloon on the end of the iron. If it is to be made into a wineglass, a blob of molten glass is added to form the stem, and this is shaped and elongated as desired by continually rolling the blowing iron with one hand and using the appropriate tools with the other. Another blob of glass is attached to the stem, and this makes the foot. It, too, is shaped with the appropriate tools. The length of the stem and width of the foot are measured as work proceeds to ensure that they are correct. The glass is then attached at the centre of its base to a rod called a pontil, and the rim is severed from the blowing iron by cooling it with water and tapping it sharply. Reheating the glass as necessary, the top of the bowl is opened out; all this being done with an appearance of the utmost casualness and ease. Yet glassmaking is a skill which takes many years to master.

The glass is broken from the pontil and, with asbestos-covered pliers, is placed in the cooling chamber, known as the lehr. The annealing process is extremely important as only by carefully controlled, gradual cooling can faults in the glass be avoided. A slowly moving belt carries the glasses through the lehr, taking about six hours on the way through. The lehr is a long oven which is hot at the beginning and is heated less and less throughout its length; when the glasses emerge they may be touched by hand.

Formerly the rim of the glass was sheared off and smoothed with great dexterity before the glass was broken from the pontil. Nowadays, with the emphasis on speed, rims are dealt with by mechanised methods. Glasses are rotated past a tungsten marker which makes an incision round the rim, the uneven top is snapped off, the edge is ground with abrasive and, finally, the glasses pass the flame from a gas jet which melts the edges just enough to smooth them.

If the glass vessel is mold-blown—and this is still a handmade glass— the blob of glass on the blowing iron is lowered into a metal mold and a lid, which fits round the blowing iron, is put on top of it. The glass is then blown until it has expanded to fit the mold. Thereafter, in the case of wine glasses, stem and foot are added in the usual way.

One astonishing feature of glass is that, once marked with a pattern or formed into a particular shape, it can be blown to a much greater size, or pulled out to enormous lengths, without losing either pattern or shape. For example, thin glass tubing, as used in thermometers, begins as a torpedo-shaped gather of hot glass, rounded on one side and V-shaped on the other, which is then stretched out to lengths of over a hundred feet. It is then a very thin tube but is still in the same pattern as it was to start with—rounded on one side, angled on the other.

This, then, is the extraordinary material we all take so much for granted. It provides a most rewarding medium for all kinds of decorative work.

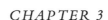

CHAPTER 3

Decorating Techniques and Choice of Glass

Methods of decorating glass can conveniently be divided into three categories. The first involves marking the surface of the glass in some way, for example by engraving or cutting; the second consists of applying a surface decoration as in painting; the third involves decorating glass with other pieces of glass, as for example in mosaic work.

One might ask, why should anyone want to decorate a glass vessel at all? After all, the glassmaker forms his glass in a particular way with a particular purpose in mind, and expects it to remain like that. The shape and size have been designed to stand alone, so why do more? Everyone will have his or her own answer to that question. Sometimes, of course, a piece of glass does undeniably have such beauty of its own that instinctively one feels that it should be left untouched. But most of the time if the decoration, in whatever way it is done, is beautiful and—above all— appropriate, I think the glass will be enhanced. But surely the best reason of all is that decorating is enjoyable, and so long as you are not ruining a costly and rare antique, why not do work which gives you pleasure? Much beautiful work survives to show that right down the ages people have enjoyed putting decoration onto glass. Some of the most attractive and skilful decoration was applied at the time of manufacture, but there has always been a wide range of techniques which have been used on glass vessels after they were made.

At the present time there are welcome signs of a revival of craft work of all kinds. It seems likely that this increase will continue as the daily lives of so many people become more and more mechanised and uncreative, and the opportunities for self-expression decrease. Many people, often without realising it, have a great urge to do creative work of some kind, but there is now hardly any chance to do this except as an activity outside one's working life. Within this general craft activity there is an encouraging revival of engraving and other ways of working on or with glass.

This revival of doing creative work has brought with it an increasing public appreciation of craftsmanship. On all sides, people are turning their attention more and more to fine, handmade articles—silver, furniture, china, glass, textiles—the list is seemingly endless. It is not only the quality which is so much appreciated in this machine-dominated age, but the evidence of the human hand at work producing a uniquely individualistic article.

ENGRAVING

Engraving appeals not only to those with an artistic flair, but also to those who have a practical nature because it involves working most of the time on articles which will be used. Of course, if you reach great heights as an engraver you will hardly expect your engraved goblets to be in daily use. Great masters of the craft use glass primarily as a means of displaying an engraving, not as a useable object to be decorated. They regard the blank glass much as a painter regards his canvas: as a support for his work.

However, most people wishing to take up engraving for their own pleasure will want to see their completed glass in use and, as I discovered, there is no knowing what this use may be. I engraved a large goblet for a friend, feeling that because of its size it would simply be displayed somewhere or perhaps used as a vase; I wondered if I should have done better to give something smaller and more useable. Then I received a worried letter: 'A terrible thing has happened. I was drinking sherry from my goblet while working at the gas cooker! It slipped from my hand and broke on the kitchen floor.'

The realisation that engraved glass is not only beautiful but highly individual has helped the revival of interest in it. There is a great satisfaction

Diamond point stipple engraved goblet with view of Airlie Castle. Designed and engraved for the wedding of Princess Alexandra, by Claire Rome

in turning an anonymous piece of glass into a personal possession. Increasingly, a piece of engraved glass is designed to mark important occasions, not only in the lives of individuals but in the history of public bodies or large organisations. For the individual, what more delightful present can be imagined than a piece of engraved glass which has been specially thought of and created for him? Even if the engraving is on a set of glasses each one will differ very slightly from the others.

Glass is a marvellous material upon which to work. It begins as a molten substance, and it seems always to keep this quality of movement. It can be amazingly sturdy, and I have certainly treated it very roughly with little thought for the hours of work I have spent on it. The only mishaps I have had were when I put some glasses on the luggage rack in a train and someone put a suitcase on them, and another occasion when I collected a pair of rather fragile goblets from an exhibition and unthinkingly put them into a hold-all with two pairs of shoes on top of them—one goblet did not survive. Glass really only needs reasonable treatment. Some people say it is best not to stand glasses upside down to drain after washing as this encourages cracks. It seems a sensible precaution.

TECHNIQUES OF ENGRAVING

Glass can be engraved by three methods: by engraving it by hand with diamond tools, by using a machine-driven copper wheel, and by an electric hand drill. Each method produces quite different effects, each with its own particular beauty and attraction and because the three methods are so different they each have their own advantages and disadvantages. Some of these are purely physical, for example lack of necessary space in which to work but, apart from any obvious pros and cons, some people with a real distaste for all machinery will automatically prefer to work only with diamond hand-tools. Those who like operating machines will go for the other types of engraving. These are, of course, judgements based on methods rather than on results, but results are likely to be much better if the method of work gives pleasure.

The only similarity between these methods of engraving is that, basically, they are all a means of scratching the surface of the glass.

In diamond point engraving the surface of the glass is marked very gently with fine diamond tools, used entirely by hand. The tools do not cut deeply into the glass, and the effect of depth has to be achieved with great delicacy. Diamond point engraving always seems to have a slight sheen or sparkle about it; this is due to the multitudes of tiny cuts made by the diamond in the surface of the glass. There is always a trace of the human hand somewhere, since no human being can be as precise as a machine. I find this an attractive and endearing characteristic of this method of engraving— a welcome reminder that people are not machines.

Copper wheel engraving, by comparison, has a cool, classical beauty. It appears to be, and indeed is, extremely precise. By comparison with diamond point engraving, it produces designs which are treated rather like sculpture, and it achieves its three-dimensional effect by sculpting the glass and by cutting it to varying depths. It is particularly suitable for any subject which responds to a sculptured effect.

Drill engraving produces a matt surface. It is possible to obtain some three-dimensional effect, but the drill does not sculpt the glass in the way that a copper wheel does. Used with skill, however, the drill can produce some quite delicate and imaginative work.

All engraving is really like drawing in reverse. Whereas in drawings the dark areas are shaded and the light areas are left untouched, in glass engraving the opposite is the case. In dark areas the glass is left untouched and in the light areas it is engraved. This takes a little getting used to, and at the first attempt at engraving it can be difficult to remember all the time that the instinctive wish to shade will produce the opposite effect from the one you want.

To a very large extent, there is no absolutely right and wrong way of engraving. This is what makes it such a pleasure to do: you are your own critic and you yourself decide what you want to create, how you want the finished work to look, and how you will set about achieving the effect you want. As far as diamond point engraving is concerned, one person will see a particular subject as a stipple engraving; another will see it as a line engraving. In copper wheel engraving one person's work will have far more interesting and inventive sculptured effects than another's. But who is to say, finally, what is 'right'? However, while you are basically free to follow your own ideas in the way you interpret a subject

D

and the methods you use, there is of course good and bad engraving. A line which should be straight may have become crooked or splintered, perhaps the stippling of a delicate area has become too heavy, or the copper wheel may have momentarily cut out of place. But, as in painting, your methods of work are all your own, and so is your interpretation of the subject.

Glass etching is a subject in itself, and is not a process suitable to use at home, involving the use of tanks of acid. Sand-blasting of glass, again, cannot be done at home. So these techniques are not covered in this book.

CHOICE OF GLASS

For engraving, the choice of glass is important. In the case of diamond point work, lead crystal undeniably gives the best all-round results. It is splendid for stippling—indeed almost essential—and engraves with good, unsplintered lines. The lead content of different makes of glass varies, consequently so does its softness; the more the lead, the softer the glass.

Soda glass, and this is the glass on which the beginner to engraving glass vessels will probably start, is the big question mark. It is so immensely varied in texture, and this is tantalising because there is a great deal of it around, the designs are often extremely attractive, and it is much cheaper than lead crystal. The only course of action is to be quite bold about this: just get some and try it: don't regret mistakes and don't mind abandoning a glass. There is so much work that can be very satisfactorily done on soda glass that it will be possible to be happily occupied with it for quite a long while before worrying too much about using lead crystal.

Once again, it is wise to buy either in small quantities, or just a single glass, until the texture of the soda glass has been tested. If it is too hard to engrave this will soon become apparent; it will feel 'unsympathetic', lines will splinter slightly, and stippling will require a decisive bang instead of a very gentle tap. But there will be a lot more soda glass available which is more suitable and even quite soft. Of course, it will never have that very special brilliance and sparkle of good lead crystal, but neither did any glass before the latter's invention. And it is as well to

Swedish crystal goblet with diamond point stipple engraving, by Barbara Norman

remember that you will probably almost always be working on soda glass when engraving a dish or plate or bowl, since these very rarely appear in the form of engravable crystal.

Another type of glass suitable for engraving in flat panels is float glass. Much modern sheet glass is now made by this method, which was invented as recently as 1959. To make float glass, molten glass is floated on a surface of liquid tin at a carefully controlled temperature. The resulting glass is very clear and needs no polishing or grinding.

A great problem is where to get glass—good glass—when you move on to lead crystal. Most lead crystal on the market is already heavily adorned by the makers, mostly as intricate cut glass. It is sometimes possible to engrave upon cut glass, but this must be very carefully considered as the cut work has already been designed to form the sole decoration. Nevertheless, an exactly appropriate diamond point design may sometimes blend in well. If difficulty is experienced in finding suitable glass to engrave it is always worthwhile approaching a manufacturer to see if he will either supply you with 'seconds' or will give a small discount if a reasonable quantity is ordered. But eventually even the prospect of a discount seems less important than just getting glass—good, plain, unadorned glass. The search for it is a challenge.

The best source of supply is usually the sales and most department stores have very good 'seconds' at sale times. These are usually by famous makers but are often unidentified by name and, if each piece is chosen with great care, all but the smallest flaws can be avoided. The flaws are often extremely difficult to detect, so that one wonders why the glass has ever been classified as a 'second' at all; however, there are some blemishes which must be looked for with particular care and avoided. The most common are air bubbles, but they may be tiny and in such a position that it does not matter from the point of view of the engraving. Sometimes, however, the air bubble may be quite large and very conspicuous. Another flaw caused by tiny bubbles is more difficult to detect. In this instance the bubbles are grouped together and are so tiny that they look like a reflection on the glass. If some bubble somewhere in the glass is unavoidable, choose a small one in an inconspicuous position such as the foot. Fine hair-lines must always be avoided: they are likely to develop into cracks. Another less common fault which is not very easy to see at first, is a scratched patch caused by bad packing. Lead crystal is very soft, and glasses must be prevented from rubbing against each other.

I have pointed out these common faults in some detail not because I think everyone else is unobservant but because until one becomes used to choosing glass for engraving there is so much to look out for. Anyway, shopping at sales time is bad enough—the light is often poor and there is nowhere to stand the piles of glasses which you have sorted through so carefully. However, it pays to persevere. Your rewards will be rich and you ought to acquire some lovely glasses.

There remains the rather difficult question of old glass: whether to engrave it or not. Most of it responds extremely well, being rather soft, but I do not much care to engrave upon it myself. This, I suppose, is partly due to a feeling of responsibility in case I spoil an irreplaceable glass, and partly due to a sentimental regard for age. This was brought home to me rather strongly when I saw a Georgian goblet which had been engraved to within an inch of its life. I wondered if it would have been possible to cram one more dot or line upon it and I immediately thought 'Well, that will never be the same again'. However, I have no doubts about using modern glass. This is not because I think it less beautiful, indeed much of it is extremely beautiful, but there is obviously much more of it around. If you engrave it well, your engraving will grow old with it until both are hallowed by age! In any case, it seems appropriate that craftsmen should primarily work on materials which are contemporary

Damaged antique glass is another matter altogether. It is sometimes possible to pick up beautiful old glasses which have small chips out of them. Do not write them off as useless. If they can possibly be used you will find them extremely good to work on and it is sometimes possible to have the surface of the glass ground so that the chip is eliminated and the glass slightly reshaped. If the glass would have been of some value in an undamaged state it is worth asking an expert restorer for an estimate for removing the chip; if the cost of having it done professionally is too high, it is sometimes possible to find someone else with the right tools who would help.

It is not usual to engrave on coloured glass, although there is nothing against using glass that is not very dark in colour. So experiment, and be prepared for some interesting results. The design will show up white because even coloured glass exhibits white cuts or scratches. The effect can be beautiful.

SURFACE DECORATION

Painting, already mentioned as an example of the surface decoration of glass, is a general term embracing a number of different techniques which are described in detail in Chapter Seven. Chapter Eight, on gold engraving under glass, deals with a very different, little known, but most interesting method of surface decoration. All these techniques, however, have one thing in common: their requirements as far as the choice of glass is concerned are very simple. Clear window glass is used for pictures and whenever else flat glass is needed, and any texture of glass vessel is suitable for unfired gilding and cold enamelling and gold engraving under glass. In these instances the hardness or softness of the glass does not matter. Sources of supply are therefore no problem and it is only necessary to choose the correct size of window glass for the picture, or to match the painted design to the shape of the glass vessel to be decorated. In the latter case, the question of design is important, as it is in engraving. However, there is now the added consideration of colour, and this can prove a most interesting form of decorative work.

APPLYING GLASS TO GLASS

It may seem that small pieces of transparent sheet glass offer little in the way of scope or interest. Yet the possibilities are immense and the results extremely beautiful, as men have recognised for thousands of years. As well as cut glass mosaic, opaque glass known as smalti can be used, as can more modern materials such as Crystal Glass Mosaic.

Fired mosaics present a totally different technique. A small electric kiln is essential but its possession opens up a long road of experiment and discovery and limitless interest. Both mosaic panelling and the molding of glass into, for example, bowls decorated with mosaic may be under-taken; glass fusing and glass forming are discussed, with mosaic work, in Chapter Nine.

With all mosaic work, choice of glass is intimately connected with the particular method of work being undertaken; this too is therefore dealt with in Chapter Nine.

CHAPTER 4

Diamond Point Engraving

I am often asked why I started to engrave glass by diamond point. The answer is simple: I saw some engraved in this way and was immediately captivated by it. However, it is perhaps more accurate to say that first of all I could not see it. A friend showed me some treasured glasses, but the light was poor and I looked in vain for the engraving—only a few faint marks were visible. I had heard so much about this engraving, about the chance discovery of an artist in an out-of-the-way village who was also an engraver, the pleasure and interest of finding such unusual and beautiful work, the commissioning of a set of glasses—and now these faint marks seemed a complete anti-climax. All this, of course, was long before I realised that diamond point engraving is an extremely delicate art, and that it should be well displayed against a dark background. If the engraving is on glasses or decanters then, of course, dark liquids like wine show up the engraving admirably. My friend had gleaned a little from the engraver about how the work was done and it sounded interesting. Eventually, faced with the need to give someone an imaginative and original present, I decided to see the artist myself and order engraved glass.

When I first really *saw* some of this diamond point engraving in a bright, well-lit studio, I realised that I had never seen anything remotely like it before. Very few people have, because it is seldom for sale commercially, being almost entirely done to private commission. Major museums on both sides of the Atlantic have a few pieces, some art exhibitions accept it, and the remainder is in private collections. I was so struck by its delicate beauty that I knew at once that I wanted to do this kind of work myself. For me, diamond point engraving far outshines all other methods. However, this is just an individual choice, and I have no wish to attempt to lessen anyone's interest in any other methods discussed in this book. I should find it greatly rewarding if the book stimulated a general interest in glass decorating as a whole, but to have played even a small part in helping forward the revival of diamond point engraving would be even better.

Diamond point engraving has an air of great lightness about it, almost a strangeness. Some time later, when I was able to give one of my own engravings to a friend, she described it as mysterious; and so it is. It is almost as if the glass is illuminated by moonlight. I always think even Laurence Whistler's engraved landscapes convey this feeling: even his country scenes in full sunlight seem to have a moonbeam air about them.

As diamond point engraving is almost wholly self-taught, finding out methods, solving problems, piecing together all available information is an absorbing task. By talking to others interested in engraving you hear different ideas. Other people's methods or solutions to problems may not suit your own way of working; but they often start a new train of thought which results in the discovery of just the method you need. All art is primarily communication, and an individual style evolves best as a result of an interchange of ideas with other artists and a knowledge of as wide a variety of work as possible. It is helpful to see as much of the work of others as possible, even if its perfection is momentarily discouraging.

Major museums in many cities, both in Europe and America, have at least a few pieces of diamond point engraved glass, although few exhibit it to advantage. In particular, the extremely delicate work of the early Dutch stipple engravers becomes almost totally invisible if exhibited against a light background—or even with no background at all, as I saw in one major museum. It was in a case in the centre of a gallery, well below eye level, a great waste of beautiful material. In addition to seeing this engraving in museums, an increasing number of art exhibitions include examples of modern work, particularly in London.

DEVELOPMENT OF HAND ENGRAVING

Hand engraved glass has extremely ancient origins. It is known that the Romans engraved glass, and although it is not certain by what means they did this, it is generally thought that they must have used very sharp flints of some kind. However, after the fall of the Roman Empire in the fifth century, which resulted in the ending of almost all artistic pursuits, there is a great gap and little more engraving appears to have been done until the sixteenth century.

By that time, as we have seen, glass manufacture had been brought to a very high level of artistic and technical achievement by the Venetians. Gradually Venetian glassmakers began to emigrate and some reached England as early as 1549. They did not settle at once, but by 1570 they had arrived in sufficient numbers to stay. Among them was Verzelini, who was granted permission by Queen Elizabeth to be the sole manufacturer for twenty-one years of Venetian-style glass in London and to teach glassmaking. He must be reckoned the first important glassmaker in England. His extremely thin glass was sometimes engraved, and the work has been identified as that of a Frenchman, Anthony de Lysle, who started as an engraver on pewter. Very few pieces of Verzelini engraved glass whose origin is accepted have survived. Other similar glass of the period, of unidentifiable maker, has come to be termed Verzelini glass simply as a means of general description.

The engraving on this early glass was done entirely by means of lines. A very firm, bold outline was drawn and the filling-in done by means of lines only. This method created some pleasing patterns, without much variation of depth; in fact, modelling was hardly attempted. Every subject was treated in the same way—animals, flowers, trees. Even the filling-in of lettering was done with very fine parallel lines, often sloping at an angle. These early Verzelini glasses were usually very fully covered with engraving, but in spite of their profusion the designs give a satisfying, harmonious impression. The general effect is bold and decisive, and full of interesting detail. Choice of subject is very varied. Apart from the flowers, trees and foliage already mentioned, there are hunting scenes, heraldic work, and intricate patterns and edgings. There is a lively air of inventiveness about it all.

The next main period of popularity for diamond point engraved glass was in Holland in the eighteenth century. Groups of cultivated people, many of them artists or poets, some simply talented amateurs, engraved for pleasure, often working in groups. In the previous century, in 1646, a woman named Anna Roemers Visscher had done the first piece of stipple engraving on a glass. However, this was only a small area of shading on a cherry; the rest of the design had been done by the line method. So even in the middle of the seventeenth century, engravers were still working wholly by means of lines.

Credit for the first real stipple engraving goes to a Dutchman of English descent, Frans Greenwood, who lived from 1680 to 1761. He was a spare-time artist who turned to diamond engraving, at first working in line and then turning entirely to stipple. His work contains many examples of closely stippled backgrounds, the whiteness of which throws up the main subject strongly. In this way, the subject was not indicated by a stippled outline, but was thrown into contrasting relief by the background.

Another Dutchman who became famous as an engraver was Aert Schouman (1710-92). His early life is unknown but he certainly studied art at some time, and then presumably turned to engraving later. By the middle of the century he was doing stipple work, some of which still survives.

The greatest of the Dutch engravers was David Wolff, who lived from 1732 to 1798. His work—entirely in stipple—is unbelievably perfect, and so delicate that it seems as if the slightest movement of air will blow it away (plate, p. 27). He was unimportant as a painter, but he acquired an immense reputation for stipple engraving. His methods were certainly very original, and rather surprising, for he is known to have struck his diamond tool with a little hammer, placing each dot separately. This method hardly conjures up in the mind the extreme delicacy of the engraving or its steam-like appearance on the glass. Wolff became so famous, and his style was so much copied, that many surviving glasses of that period whose creators cannot be identified are called 'Wolff glasses' as a general indication of the type of engraving. Wolff's engravings differ from Greenwood's in that he concentrates on his main subjects, stipples outlines where they are needed, and leaves his backgrounds rather dark and mysterious, faintly stippling them in half-tones. It is just as if his subjects have stepped forward into the light.

Dutch engravers acquired a great reputation, far beyond the boundaries of their own country. They tended to engrave glass from other countries rather than to make their own; thus there grew up a considerable trade with England in the course of which glasses from Newcastle were exported to Holland to be engraved by Dutch engravers. Surviving pieces of Newcastle glass, engraved in Holland, are collectors' pieces today.

All these Dutch stipple engravings leave one spellbound by their absolute perfection. They are technically astonishing, too, because it is extremely difficult to achieve work so fine that no separate dots in the stippling can be seen. One cannot hope to produce work like this, and one regrets one's own inadequacy, so it was a real relief to come upon enlarged photographs of some of Wolff's stippling and to see that under the magnifying glass there really *are* individual dots and—even greater relief—that some of them are very slightly out of place. Nevertheless, with the naked eye there is not a dot to be seen—only a filmy vapour on the glass.

Parallel with the work of the Dutch engravers of the eighteenth century, there was an interesting development taking place in England in the subject matter for engraved glass. At the time of the efforts of the Stuarts to regain the English throne many Jacobite societies flourished, and it was the custom of some of them to use drinking glasses engraved with Jacobite emblems and verses from the illegal Jacobite hymn, ending with 'Amen'. Very few genuine examples of these 'Amen Glasses' still exist, although there have been many forgeries.

Following upon the Jacobite glasses were Williamite glasses, which were engraved to celebrate the victory of William of Orange at the Battle of the Boyne in 1690. Again, only a few genuine examples have survived. But the custom was growing of celebrating important events with commemorative pieces of engraved glass.

The present revival of diamond point engraving in England was started in the mid-1930s by William Wilson and Laurence Whistler, independently of each other. Both are self-taught. William Wilson's work is principally in the field of lettering and in the design of elegant presentation pieces. Laurence Whistler has developed a very distinctive style of stipple engraving, stronger than that of the Dutch engravers of the eighteenth century. Interest in this work is increasing and the number of people who turn to diamond point engraving grows steadily. In Holland, too, there is a revival of the craft.

In the United States the Steuben glassworks sometimes combine diamond point engraving with their magnificent wheel engraving, using it where special effects of lightness are required such as cloud vapour, stars, and so on. In America, too, as in Europe, an increasing number of private patrons and large institutions are commissioning work.

ADVANTAGES OF DIAMOND POINT ENGRAVING

This method of engraving has so many advantages and pleasures. It needs very little equipment: basically, a diamond and a piece of glass—crystal glass for the finest work. But I find that the mention of such lavish words as 'diamond' and 'crystal' fill people with apprehension—they sound wildly extravagant, hardly part of everyday life, certainly not things you go out and buy casually. I find, too, that people are, not unnaturally, quite unable to visualise what the diamonds look like, nor do they know where they can be bought. After all, they do not appear to be displayed anywhere; in fact, I have never seen any on view myself. They have to be sought out painstakingly, or ordered direct from the manufacturers. But there is no real need to be intimidated by these two words.

Another great advantage of diamond point engraving is that it is a sociable occupation. It does not have to be done in a workshop, nor need the engraver retreat into isolation. Provided the work is not of too intricate a nature, it is possible to work in comfort in an armchair while listening to the radio. The engraver must just be sure that the nerves of any companions are steady enough not to mind the gentle tapping and scraping sounds that will inevitably be made. If they do mind, then perhaps they could be made sufficiently interested in the work to take up engraving themselves! After all, the Dutch in past centuries found this an agreeable occupation for groups of friends.

Storage of working material and finished work is no problem either. Surely everyone must be able to find room somewhere for a few glasses?

As one who lives in a flat and who has turned to engraving from oil painting, it is an enormous relief not to have to struggle to avoid brushing past a wet canvas for several days on end; and a strong smell of linseed oil and turpentine penetrating into every room is not always the most agreeable thing in the world. In a way, painting is a more solitary means of self-expression. Primarily you paint something which you yourself want to express and, because it is such an individual conception, it is not certain that anyone else will like it, or even begin to understand what you are trying to say. It is very much more likely that your engravings will give pleasure to a great many people, and this in itself is a means of communication.

I think the reasons why engraved glass is usually well liked are varied. For one thing, you are not immediately up against people's very deeply rooted prejudices concerning the use of colour. A great many people seem to be nervous and unsure of their own judgement when choosing a painting. They are seldom sure about what they are looking for, and frequently make an emotional choice (or rejection) based to a large extent on the colours used. An engraving can, at least, be chosen without running up against this problem. Another thing is that engravings have a very special beauty and interest which is not captured by any other medium. But I often think that one of the main reasons why engraved glass is so widely appreciated is that it can be *used*. People are reluctant to commit themselves to buying anything in the way of art which can only be looked at. This is a pity, but perhaps the reluctance to spend money on something not intended for use lingers on from more puritanical times. This does, however, help more than one art-form, including engraved glass.

Engraving has, I believe, much greater individuality than painting. It is all too easy for an amateur painter to imitate the style of another painter, even if subconsciously. How often, for example, can Cézanne's distinctive landscape colours be seen in the work of others, how many imitators have other Impressionists had? But it is extremely difficult to capture the style of another engraver. To begin with, there are no colours to copy; but above all it is impossible to imitate exactly the delicacy, or the strength, of another person's touch. You may choose the same subject but, however slightly, the force with which your diamond meets the glass will be different from that used by anybody else. And as engraving cannot be altered, an individual instinctive style will inevitably be developed.

Of all forms of engraving, diamond point work is most akin to drawing. People often say, hopelessly, that they cannot draw, and are therefore absolutely certain that they could never engrave. Yet, clearly, there is a feeling stirring that they would like to do so. Of course, there is no denying that it helps greatly to be able to draw, but I firmly believe that to a large extent drawing is based on observation, and above all on practice. So a fear of not being able to draw, or a reluctance to try, should not be allowed to stand in the way of engraving. If however you really cannot draw, no matter how simply, there are plenty of other ways of engraving. The most obvious is lettering (see p. 81). Another type of subject which does not need a talent for creative drawing is geometrical design. The symmetry of this kind of subject greatly appeals to some temperaments. Either of these might restore the confidence of the timid, though I believe that, once launched upon the fascinating work of engraving, fears vanish. Suddenly you can see in your mind just the thing you want to engrave: it involves drawing, so you just start work and draw it.

Another fear which people seem to have about starting to engrave is that they think it is finicky work and that it demands a fussy, pedantic mind. That is very far from true. What it does demand is good planning, and the ability to make a decision and keep to it—the very opposite of fussy, which implies a preoccupation with unnecessary little details. Engraving needs a broad vision, a complete assessment of the whole problem through every stage, a firmness of intention. You cannot be vague or sketchy. You must see it all before you start work and then, having taken your decisions about placing and methods, you must carry them through in the right order. Mistakes can never be undone, although they may sometimes be disguised.

There is another common misapprehension about the nature of the work. 'Surely', people say, 'you have to be tremendously patient. I couldn't possibly do it'. I am quite sure it does not demand patience— at least not in the slow, plodding way that the questioners always imply. The work moves along amazingly quickly, and how can you have that

Swedish plate with diamond point line-and-stipple engraving, by Barbara Norman

E

slow kind of patience when you are fired with the interest of the emerging design? One moment you have before you a blank piece of glass, a drawing of your design, and a few tools. Then you take the plunge and make the first marks. It is too late now to turn back or change your mind, you must work steadily on, and with surprising speed the design takes shape.

SUBJECTS FOR ENGRAVING

The choice of subjects suitable for hand engraving is almost limitless, offering as it does such scope in the way of interpretation. It is worth repeating that all glass started as a moving substance and in a subtle way seems to retain this sense of mobility. This, I believe, is why flowers, foliage and other growing things are particularly suitable subjects; indeed, for many centuries they have been the principal ones. Some people see flowers and plants of all kinds as an obviously feminine choice of material. I think they often (though admittedly not always) mistake the artist's intentions and point of view. I myself enjoy painting and engraving flowers not because they are sentimentally pretty but because they have a robust vitality. In fact, I do not find flowers pretty at all; I simply feel that they are alive and full of character and it is this living quality that I try to portray. However, if you do feel that they are pretty this will probably be unconsciously revealed in your treatment of them.

Animals and birds make marvellous subjects for diamond point engraving, but particularly birds. There is infinite variety in feathers, and the treatment of them is a great challenge. I think they can be more interestingly portrayed in diamond point than in any other kind of engraving. If the piece of engraved glass is destined for a particular person, an animal or bird can often be chosen for its special significance. This adds greatly to the interest of the piece of engraving. Fish, which have useful and adaptable curves and fins, are another very pleasing subject. Coats of arms are an obvious subject—but extremely difficult and usually very intricate. To add to the obvious difficulties, the specimen one is given to work from is so often about the size of a postage stamp. Lettering, geometrical designs, patterns invented from casual scribblings,

Coat of arms of Guy's Hospital engraved by diamond point on Swedish crystal, by Claire Rome

Swedish crystal bowl with diamond point line-and-stipple engraving, by Barbara Norman

Pilkington float-glass panel, 20in × 16in, engraved on both sides with diamond point engraving, by Claire Rome

landscapes, buildings, ships, all these and countless more are possibilities
if you have a steady hand and a good eye.

Perhaps a more widespread effort to portray some aspects of contemporary life would be a good thing. After all, if the engraving survives,
future generations may be as interested to see two twentieth-century
astronauts or a scene from a football match as we are to see scenes from
the daily life of former centuries.

FINDING SUBJECTS

Obviously the greatest pleasure and satisfaction is gained by searching out
a chosen subject at source. If it is to be a plant or flower, what better than
to find a growing one and make your drawing from that? If you have in
mind an animal or bird, a living specimen provides the greatest scope for
originality of treatment. However, this kind of on-the-spot research is not
always possible. It is useless to wish for a summer flower in December,
and if the subject is an animal this can so often only be seen in a zoo
which may offer little opportunity for action sketches. The next best
thing is to consult the best reference books possible. Get a good botanical
book which shows accurately exactly how your chosen plant grows,
how many petals its flowers have, where the leaves are spaced. Try to
discover as thoroughly as possible what its character is so that in the
process of adaptation it will not be made to look uncomfortable on the
glass. Similarly, any natural history book should be a good one which
will show animals in their right proportions and in typical surroundings.
In order to make the animal fit the glass and to portray it in a natural
position several books may have to be consulted, and the design built up
in this way.

When starting to engrave you will be very tempted to try to make
exact copies from illustrations in books. Fortunately, this is extremely
difficult as the illustrations are seldom the right size, the flowers are
growing in the wrong direction, or the animals won't begin to fit the
glass. This will force you to be creative and to make a design of your own
choice to fit that particular piece of glass. This serves as a reminder of
what I said previously about the inescapable individuality of engraving.

Swedish crystal goblet with diamond point stipple engraving, by Barbara Norman

No two people will create exactly the same design from a botanical drawing; they will each discover the characteristics of the plant, and then they will each produce an entirely different design for same shaped glass.

EQUIPMENT NEEDED

ENGRAVING TOOLS

There is a wide variety of tools for hand engraving, made either of diamonds or steel. Some engravers use both, as the need arises. Some never use anything but diamonds, and feel that nothing cuts the surface of the glass so well and so cleanly. Others feel that steel tools allow greater fluency of line.

Diamond Tools.   Diamond tools are most commonly obtainable in three basic types. The simplest, and therefore cheapest, is a tiny piece of diamond set in the tip of a wooden holder. The most usual use for this type of tool, which is called a writing diamond, is in science or industry whenever there is a need to write on a glass container or slide. These tiny diamonds have distinct cutting edges.

The first thing to learn is that diamond tools are usually held vertically and not at a slope like a pen. If one of these writing diamonds is held in one particular way it will scarcely mark the surface of the glass, or in some cases will not mark it at all. If the tool is turned round, various cutting edges will become apparent—usually one very good one and others less good but suitable for general filling in. If the tool has no distinguishing mark, such as a maker's name, on the handle to help you to find the cutting edge easily, it is useful to put some sort of mark on it.

These simple diamond tools are a pleasure to work with and are capable of producing extremely good work if skilfully used. Obviously, most people will eagerly want to progress to better (and therefore more expensive) ones, but if this cannot be afforded do not let it be a discouragement. If you keep to designs which best suit the simple tools you will meet few problems. However, if they are used for lettering there will inevitably be difficulties. The reason for this is that the diamond is only a tiny piece

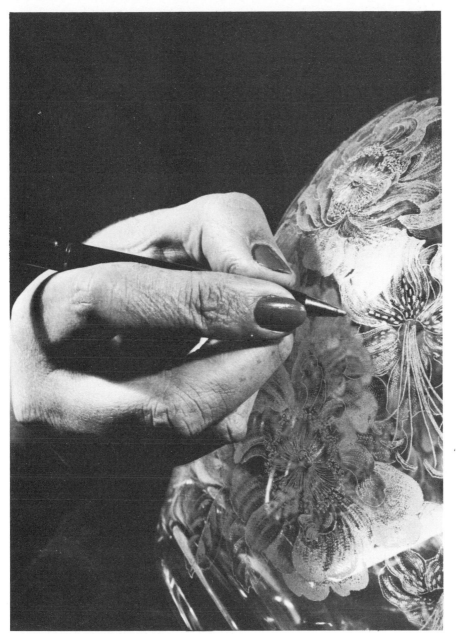

Claire Rome using the Lunzer Lancer engraving tool

and not a point, as a pen or pencil would be. Therefore, when holding the tool vertically in position the diamond itself is not visible, and in any outline where you need to take a line back to join its beginning it is extremely difficult to achieve the join accurately if you cannot see exactly the position of the diamond. Difficult, but not impossible. However, they are excellent tools for all straightforward line work, and for simple stippling too.

Working upwards in cost, the next type of diamond tool is another small piece of diamond. This time it is a 'long' piece, about one-eighth of an inch in length. It is usually set in a very lightweight plastic holder of the type used for ballpoint pens, and is therefore light and easy to use. These long chips also have various edges, some extremely sharp and suitable for lines, some much less so, and some almost non-cutting. As in the case of the writing diamonds, it is very helpful and time-saving if the holder can be marked with a guide to the sharpest edge. With a good specimen of one of these long diamond tools it is really possible to undertake any kind of work. Because the diamond protrudes from the holder it is possible to see exactly where it is on the surface of the glass. Therefore they are quite suitable for lettering, as well as for both line and stipple. These tools are splendid all-rounders, and if they eventually become chipped too much for use in delicate line work, they are then often very useful for filling in by a gentle scratching stroke.

The third type of diamond tool is once again usually set in a wooden holder, but is more expensive than the other two kinds. The diamond does not look remotely like a diamond as it is black; nor does it even feel sharp to the touch. The point is conical, and the tool looks rather like a neatly sharpened pencil. The holders and metal mounts are beautifully made, and it is something to use with great care. This kind of tool is heavier than either of the other two but, being so well made, it is not in the least tiring to use. These diamonds have the great advantage that if they become blunt or chipped they can be sharpened by the makers. Each time this is done, however, some of the diamond is ground away—in fact, rather an alarming amount disappears, so try not to have it done more than about twice. Perhaps some tools might stand three sharpenings.

Many people will want to know the cost of diamond tools. At a time of constantly rising prices and fluctuating foreign exchange rates it is not possible to be precise. The price range of the tools is very wide, but as a rough guide a simple writing diamond can be bought for about the same price as a medium-grade ballpoint pen. A very good diamond tool costs approximately the same as a luxury ball-point. Above that, the cost is high and the tools are very specialised and are often made to the individual designs of craftsmen.

Steel Tools. Steel (tungsten carbide) tools can be rather difficult to track down to a source of supply. It is probably best if a small engineering firm can be found which is willing to make a limited quantity. If such a firm has not already done this for an engraver they may not understand exactly what is needed and they will have to be given a detailed description. If you have not seen one either—which is likely to be the case—there will be difficulties on both sides, so the following rough outline may be helpful.

I have discovered two kinds of tungsten tools so far. The first has a fine, and exceedingly sharp, point. This point is about the same shape and size as gramophone needles were when they existed. For those who don't remember such things, I can perhaps best describe the piece of metal by saying that it is like half an inch of lead from a pencil. In my case the firm concerned mounted the tips in the kind of lightweight holders used for ballpoint pens. These tools are splendid for fine outlines and for lettering. For stippling they tend to be a little too finely pointed, although where very tiny dots are needed they can be used very successfully. The other kind of metal tip is made for me by another firm, who supply only the unmounted tips in quantities of half a dozen. All that is then needed is a simple, but very firm, clutch-type pencil holder which can be bought from any good art shop or stationer.

BLACK VELVET

One other piece of equipment which is just as essential under all circumstances as diamond tools is a piece of black velvet. This is either used to place the piece of glass on so that the design can be clearly seen without any reflection, or it can be put inside the glass. If the engraving goes round the glass it will be necessary to put the velvet inside in order to avoid the reflection of what has already been engraved on the further side.

EQUIPMENT FOR PUTTING DESIGNS ON GLASS

Certain equipment is essential for putting designs on to glass before engraving can be started. The various methods and their advantages and drawbacks are discussed in detail on page 000, but the equipment itself will be any or all of the following:

    Pencil suitable for writing on glass (referred to in future as a wax pencil)
    White chalk pencil for drawing on paper
    Graphite pencil for drawing on glass
    White poster paint
    Very fine watercolour brush
    Gum arabic powder
    Powdered yellow or white paint
    Tracing paper
    Tracing pencil (this has a very hard lead)
    Pencil with a very hard coloured lead, capable of being sharpened to a
        fine point
    Small pot of liquid glue (soluble in water)

I will not list other desirable and useful items at this stage as it would be confusing until the need for them can be understood. When you have tried some engraving you will soon know which of the suggested items of equipment you really need.

When getting the watercolour brush it is only necessary to buy a squirrel hair one; sable is much more expensive and is not needed. It is very useful indeed to have a brush with a sharp point at the end of the handle. As regards the wax pencil, there are several makes on the market. Try some before choosing, and get the one that makes the finest lines which can be rubbed off most easily with a finger-tip without leaving too much greasy deposit. Some pencils make rather thick lines. A white wax pencil is the most useful all-round colour, but it is wise to have another colour too for indicating measurement marks. Red or yellow both show up well on glass.

LIGHTING

Lighting may, perhaps, be included as equipment. It is essential to be able to see your work very clearly so, if you are working by daylight, be as near a window as possible. Artificial light presents more problems as it creates tiresome reflections on the glass, and shadows are cast by hand and tool. I find it essential to work with an adjustable, angled reading lamp. Overhead lighting causes quite unmanageable reflections and only by using something adjustable can these be counteracted. Use the kind of lamp that can be moved and twisted to all heights and in all directions; it will then be just as effective standing on the floor while you are seated in an armchair and engraving. Some engravers say that the light should be so placed that it shines directly into the bowl of a glass, but obviously the best position is simply the one which causes the least reflection.

POSTURE

Before you begin to do any hand engraving, a few words about posture may be helpful in saving a great deal of discomfort. Whether you are working at a table, or on your lap while sitting in an upright chair, or in an armchair, you will find that you easily get stiffness in neck, shoulders or arms—or in all three. This is understandable because one hand will be grasping a fairly small object very tightly, and the other will be holding a very thin tool, usually with an unnecessarily tense grip. And if, as is more than likely, you become totally absorbed in your work, you may be in this cramped position for rather a long time; the result will be a sort of widespread writer's cramp in every imaginable muscle. So stop work at intervals, relax and move arms and neck to exercise the muscles. Many aches and pains will be avoided.

GLASS FRAGMENTS

Perhaps I ought to mention glass fragments. You cannot keep scratching and tapping at glass without making a lot of little chippings, all with extremely sharp edges. It is easy to overlook this. So be careful what happens to all these pieces and do not scatter them. It will frequently be necessary to brush them from the work, and for those with a delicate or sensitive skin it is advisable to use a brush or a piece of cloth to do this. Personally, I have found the fragments harmless to my hands, but I know others who have been caused much discomfort by them. Protection of one's eyes is important. If you do not wear spectacles (which give good protection) take great care not to get too close to your work.

METHODS USED

LINE

Line engraving which some engravers prefer to use exclusively, consists only of lines of varying length and strength. The best examples of this method are to be found on engraved Verzelini glasses of the sixteenth century. Every effect of light and shade is obtained simply by lines. In areas where the whiteness of the engraving is to be faded out this is achieved by finer and finer strokes, spaced further and further apart, and probably diminishing in length too. This method of engraving has great charm, but its simplicity is deceptive because it requires much inventiveness. It is particularly suitable for subjects from nature such as birds (showing feathers well when done very finely), animals (where it can distinguish between the varying textures of fur), or plants and flowers. The delightful modern engravings of Felix White show this method at its best. Line engraving is also very useful in heraldic subjects.

STIPPLE

Stippling is the other main method of hand engraving. This consists of a

English crystal goblet with diamond point stipple engraving, by Barbara Norman

vast number of tiny dots, delicately made with a very fine diamond point. Maximum lightness (or brightness) is obtained by placing the dots extremely close together and by using the tool with greater emphasis. The dots (and consequently the brightness) are faded out either by using decreasing pressure, which requires great skill and control, or by combining this with increasing the space between the dots. When doing stipple engraving, you may either draw a delicate outline and then fill it in with stippling or, if you want to keep solely to the stipple method, you may make the outline by means of closely placed dots too. To achieve a sharp outline by stippling will test skill to its limit. For outlining, each dot must be placed separately and not done at speed.

There is another kind of stipple engraving, practised on occasion by Frans Greenwood, which needs great skill. With this method the subject is outlined very finely with dots, and the background is then stippled round it, leaving the subject as a silhouette. The background stippling is closest (and therefore whitest) where it is outlining the subject. Then— and this is what calls for such skill—it is very gently faded out until it vanishes into nothing. The stipple-outlined subject can then be dealt with very simply, either by continuing with the stipple method to work out the details, or by using line work. The contrast of the methods can be effective.

A variation of this method—beautiful, but calling for a great deal of work—is not to fade out the background stippling at all, but to cover the whole of the rest of the glass with it, all at the same intensity. The design then appears in silhouette upon what seems to be a delicately frosted glass.

The action of stippling can be very rapid. In his book *Engraved Glass 1952-1958*, Laurence Whistler says that the rate of his strokes is eight per second. It is interesting to contrast this with the great Dutchman, Wolff, who worked with his little hammer, placing each dot separately and meticulously. Surely this must have been an exceedingly slow method? It is important to realise that there is no correct speed of work. Each person must work at the speed which he finds produces the best results.

COMBINING LINE AND STIPPLE

Many engravers use a combination of both line and stipple. It is not possible to give a precise guide when to change from one to another, but it is essential to decide this as part of the detailed preliminary planning of the engraving.

STARTING WORK

PUTTING A DESIGN ON GLASS

Now that the basic equipment has been assembled and there is some knowledge of the various engraving techniques, a start can be made on actual work. First choose some simple pattern, perhaps something geometrical, or foliage—anything with good lines. Make a preliminary drawing with the white chalk on a piece of black paper. It is almost always necessary to make preliminary drawings of any design. If these are done on black paper with a white chalk pencil the question of shaded and unshaded (or, to be exact, engraved and unengraved) areas can be worked out at the drawing stage. In fact, it is helpful to make drawings of suitable subjects as and when ideas occur. In this way, a book of designs can be built up. It can save a lot of effort if, at a time when ideas are scarce, you can browse through your own design book.

Having made your preliminary drawing, try out the various methods of putting the design onto the glass. It is very useful to begin with a piece of plain picture glass, which can be bought cheaply. Before you start, put passe-partout or adhesive tape round the edges—glass is sharp.

By Wax and Graphite Pencils.   First, use the method of drawing the design on the glass with the wax pencil, keeping the pencil point very sharp. This is a good method for those who work easily with a pencil, the only slight disadvantage is that it is difficult to keep the outlines as fine as you would like them to be. There is a small point to observe concerning wax pencils. Contrary to what I had been told and, indeed, to what I had read, these pencils do not mark best on clean glass but on glass which has been well handled. This is because the slight grease from one's hand acts on the wax as a softener. The opposite is true of graphite pencils made for writing on glass or plastic. These require an absolutely

F

clean surface: it is then possible to draw very fine lines on the glass with them and this method of putting on the design should now be tried.

By Painting.   Having tried out the wax or graphite pencil method, try painting on the design. Some people prefer this method because they find working with a brush produces an easier flow of line. Moisten the white poster paint slightly, using water, and paint on the design as delicately as possible; the lines will nevertheless generally prove to be too thick. This is when the pointed brush handle comes in useful. Give the paint a few minutes to dry, then gently scrape some of it away with the brush handle until the line has been reduced to a hair's breadth. This has the added advantage of enabling the shape of an outline to be slightly corrected. (I have suggested using a brush with a pointed handle simply because it saves one more piece of equipment, but obviously something like an orange stick would do equally well.)

When working on the engraving, you may become so absorbed in the work that you rub off large areas of the painted design with your hands. This can always be painted on again or retouched, of course, but it only creates more work. So if you find this happening it would be best to use the liquid glue instead of water to moisten the poster paint, giving it a little longer to dry. Outlines made with this can also be gently scraped to the desired fineness once they are completely dry.

By Tracing.   Another method of putting designs on glass is to make a drawing of the design on tracing paper then, with a pin, prick carefully round the design. Fix this piece of perforated paper very securely to the glass, using transparent adhesive tape to hold it and ensuring that the paper is very tightly stretched over the glass. Then, using a soft paintbrush, dust all over the pricked-out design with a mixture of equal parts of dry, powdered gum arabic and powdered paint. Make sure that the powdered mixture sifts through all the pin pricks in the tracing paper. Then breathe several times on to it, wait a minute or two, and carefully peel off the tracing paper. A dotted outline of the design will be left on the glass, the dampness of your breath having moistened the gum arabic in the powder mixture.

I always find it helpful, indeed often essential, to remove the painted or drawn outline as work progresses. This is easily done for any of the methods described above. Just rub the outlines off with a finger tip. If white paint or pencil is left on the glass too long it is impossible to judge what method should be used in the next stages of the work if what you have done is partly blurred by no longer useful pencil outlines.

By Poster Paint and Lead Pencil.   If it has been found that drawing comes more easily on glass with a pencil than with a brush, the following method might be found even more suitable. Using poster paint moistened with liquid glue instead of water, paint over a large area of the glass. When the paint is thoroughly dry, a well sharpened soft pencil may be used to draw the design. (It is important to use only a very soft pencil in direct contact with lead glass as this kind of glass scratches very easily.) This method of drawing with a soft lead pencil has the advantage that an eraser can be used so that corrections may be made. If a light is then so placed that it shines directly into the bowl of the glass while you are working, the engraving will show up well as the work proceeds. The disadvantage of this method is that it obscures the delicacy of the engraving while work is in progress. The paint should be washed off as soon as practicable.

Using a Drawing as a Guide.   Now another exercise can be tried out. So far, the designs have either been painted on to the glass, or drawn on by various methods. Some engravers prefer to put a drawing of the design inside a glass and to use this as their guide. In effect they are tracing the design from a piece of paper straight on to the glass, but using engraving tools to do so. This method requires great care as allowances must continually be made for the distortion of the design as seen through the glass. However, to try the method out under the simplest conditions, put a drawn design under a sheet of glass. It is then possible to appreciate the demands this method makes upon hand and eye. Nevertheless, some people prefer it.

ENGRAVING ON PICTURE GLASS

Having decided which method you prefer for putting your design on to glass, start work on line engraving. Always remember that diamonds are very fragile and break and chip easily. This sounds unlikely, but it is so: within an hour of starting engraving I had broken the point of an expensive diamond. Of course as a beginner I should not have used such a tool, but I lacked advice and instruction, as the majority of people do when they begin this work. So only use the cheaper writing diamond on sheet glass.

Holding the tool vertically above the glass, draw the outline of your design. Turn the tool round slightly if you do not at once find the cutting edge. Fill in, by means of closely placed short strokes, the area which you have shown as white on your drawing. Fade out to dark areas by spacing the strokes increasingly far apart and making them shorter. Leave dark areas blank. Try different subjects with this method. Discover how to treat feathers and fur, and how to represent hard surfaces and curved surfaces.

Next try a mixture of stippling and line. Say you have chosen to engrave a flower: draw the outline finely. Fill in the light parts of the pattern with stippling. Work very delicately and do not give way to the temptation to bang upon the glass. However, as sheet glass is hard this is intended merely as an exercise in the method of stippling; you will not achieve a delicate effect or get much difference in texture as the stippling is faded out.

If the limitations of picture glass are borne in mind, it will nevertheless often be found a useful way of working out a difficult design. You will always know that you cannot get the variety of tone and texture which you will be achieving on good lead crystal, but you will find it extremely helpful to use a piece of picture glass much as a rough note pad.

Do not cut down the time spent on the practice work outlined above. It is valuable because it provides an opportunity to become accustomed to using a diamond tool and to get the feel of working on glass. Broaden out with an increasing range of designs and experiment with the wide variety of effects which can be obtained.

WORKING ON GLASSES

When you feel ready to venture on to a glass, as opposed to sheet glass, for the sake of economy get soda glass and use line engraving to start with. This will accustom you to the problems of choosing a suitable design for a curved surface and of placing a design in a limited space. Now that your interest is aroused, you will be constantly looking at glass to see how a particular goblet or bowl or wineglass could be engraved. It is hard to say which step is first: choosing the glass shape and then getting an idea for the design, or having an idea already simmering in your mind and then seeing the piece of glass that is just right for it. But whichever way it happens, this fitting together of glass and design is an immensely enjoyable discovery.

The placing of a design is very important, and this first part of the work should not be rushed. Much will depend upon the shape of the glass you have chosen. If the design fits easily on to the glass there will be no problems of margin, and you will only have to see that you have placed it to your satisfaction. If, however, you have a design which is rather large you must take care to leave about half an inch free above it or it will not look right. It must not be lost in a desert of bare glass, nor be crowded into too small a space. This is particularly important if the design is to stand alone and is not part of an overall pattern.

The base of a glass presents problems. The glass is always thicker at the base—sometimes extremely thick—and there are problems of distortion which vary with each different design of glass. You must consider carefully how far down into this distorted area you will take your design. Sometimes it is evident that it must be avoided altogether and the size of the design must be adjusted accordingly. Sometimes, however, the distorted part of the glass is incorporated into the design intentionally to achieve certain effects. It can, for example, be used to create an illusion of water.

If at this point you feel any doubts about the design which has just been painted or drawn on the glass and cannot visualise it in a finished state, use the wax pencil to shade it in as it will be engraved. This gives a good rough visual idea of how the engraving will look.

Before starting to engrave, it is essential to pause and consider the design in all aspects—placing, size, modelling. The work of putting it on to the glass has been small-scale and detailed; there should now be a moment when, metaphorically, you stand back and view it in its entirety, relating it to its environment. If the impression it creates is not entirely satisfactory, rub the drawing off the glass and start again. Anything that displeases or jars at the drawing stage will be much worse when it has been engraved. Decide, before making the first marks upon the glass, in exactly what order the engraving is to proceed and how this or that potential difficulty will be overcome. This will save much dismay later on.

Now do your engraving. You cannot tell until you actually start work on a glass with an engraving tool just how soft and responsive it is. If you find that the soda glass on which you are working is fairly soft this is very fortunate, because it can be used for your first serious attempt at stippling. If the glass is found to be rather hard, you will certainly have to find something softer for stipple work, otherwise your tools will soon be ruined.

The methods of putting the design on to glass which have already been described apply equally to stippling, of course, so first get the design on to the glass. Now you can either draw a delicate outline with a diamond, or you can attempt an all-stippled design. If you choose the latter method, the outline must be meticulously made with closely placed, fine dots. You will probably not be able to put these on at speed as in the case of the main stippling, but will put them on individually as if you were making a careful dotted line with a pencil. When you have outlined the design by either method, stipple in the light and shade. Work with great delicacy.

Having now done designs by line only and by stipple only, the next step is to combine both methods in the same design, and this combined method is probably the one you will most often use. Part of the great interest of hand engraving, at least to me, is the preliminary thoughts and ideas you have about the method you want to use for a particular design. Indeed, preliminary thought and decision is absolutely essential. It is no use launching off into a piece of engraving, using stipple and then wishing you had done that part in line, or using lines and then regretting their decisive hardness and visualising the softer effect of stipple. Sometimes design and method both become clear at the same moment. You get an idea for a design and at once know that it is to be done in a particular way. Sometimes the design appeals greatly to you but it is difficult to decide how a certain effect, which you can see clearly enough in your mind, is to be achieved. This is where your past failures come in so useful. You are bound to spoil something sooner or later; do not throw it away in disgust for you will be very grateful for every fraction of its surface for practice purposes.

MORE ADVANCED WORK

The methods of work described above, and the vast amount of possible designs available, will provide most people with work for a considerable time. However, there are many more types of work to be learned and methods to try.

MEASURING

At this stage of development, it is essential to be able to solve the many problems connected with making accurate measurements on glasses with sloping sides to enable straight lines to be drawn. When starting on engraving it can be very reassuring to have some methods of measuring upon which to fall back when necessary. A blank glass surface, often shaped or curving in some way, can be very daunting. You may always want to use some of these methods (or you may invent others), or with greater experience you may be able to place designs faultlessly simply by training yourself to do so. The need will often arise for making accurate measurements round a glass, for drawing vertical straight lines on it or for drawing a continuous line or lines round its circumference. All this can, of course, be done by measuring with a piece of card and a ruler, but a marker can be a great help.

Simple Markers.   What is needed to make a marker is some small, simple kind of flat surface on which can be drawn a circle with a diameter of about four inches, with an upright rod fixed beside it. An adjustable clip which can hold a pencil firmly should be attached to the upright rod. The circle already drawn should be marked off with a series of circles of decreasing diameter. If these are placed closely enough together they will correspond in size to the rims of a great variety of glasses. Divide the circles into several equal parts—sixteen is a geometrically convenient number. If a glass is now placed upside down on the marked surface to correspond with one of the circles, it is possible to make accurate measurements round its rim.

When it is necessary to draw a line horizontally round a glass, fix a wax pencil firmly in position in the holder attached to the upright rod and mark the position on the glass where the line is to be. Adjust the pencil to the right height, stand the glass on the flat working surface so that it just makes contact with the pencil, then revolve the glass slowly. An accurate, unwavering line will thus be drawn. To mark a vertical line, the pencil attached to the marker can be moved up or down the vertical rod, holding the glass against it.

If you have no means of making a marker along the lines of the one described, it is perfectly possible to measure accurately in another way. To make measured divisions round the rim of a glass first draw round the rim on a piece of paper. Find the centre of this circle by measuring with a ruler. Then use a protractor to divide the circle into the required number of divisions. To mark a horizontal line round a glass, first decide how far down from the rim the line is to be, cut a strip of thin card a little longer than this and about half an inch wide (a strip from a postcard will do). Put the narrow end of the card on a level with the rim of the glass and then mark on the card the position of the line. Keeping the edge of the card carefully level with the rim, make a series of carefully placed dots on the glass with a wax pencil. Remove the card and join the dots together to make a straight line. To make a vertical line, fix the long edge of the strip of card securely to the glass with transparent tape, ensuring that the narrow end exactly fits the rim. Then use the vertical edge of the card as a guide for drawing the line.

It should be noted that the methods of engraving vertical lines so far described apply only to lines on straight-sided glasses or to very short lines on curved ones. The limitations of long vertical lines on curved glasses is dealt with on page 84.

Flexible Cord.   There is another method of establishing a guide line which has both advantages and disadvantages; it must be used with discernment to get the most from it. The material concerned is flexible cord, as used by draughtsmen. It is generally sold in lengths of twelve or eighteen inches, and is really a piece of plastic piping which can be bent into any shape and will then retain that shape. Equally, it can be completely straightened again. This is a great advantage. The only slight drawback is that it is fairly heavy.

The cord will bend to fit the shape of a glass, and may be fixed to the glass, at a measured distance from the rim, with cellulose tape. As the same piece of cord will be used over and over again, do not cut it into short lengths; instead, lap the ends over each other, not alongside each other. A line can then be drawn round the glass, using the cord as a guide. If one is very confident, the line may be engraved straight away. There will be small gaps, of course, where the cord has been fixed to the glass, but these can be filled in when it has been removed.

Another very valuable use for the cord is in drawing and engraving circles or ovals around curved surfaces, for example on a decanter which curves both horizontally and vertically. The cord can be bent into the desired shape, and then pressed into position on the curved surface of the glass.

It is problems like these and the overcoming of them which makes engraving such an absorbing occupation. The methods of measuring and marking described above have been most helpful to me, and to others.

LETTERING

Having devised satisfactory means of measuring, lettering will undoubtedly come high on the list of new work to be undertaken. This subject, however, deserves some general thought before one launches into it. To engrave lettering is difficult and mistakes are all too easy to make; but it must be mastered as it is not only often a necessary part of a design but it adds greatly to the interest of an engraving in after years.

Calligraphy is a beautiful and very precise art, and just because of its precision I think there is perhaps a tendency to overlook its individuality. It demands such discipline in execution that there has grown up a general idea that it must undeviatingly be done in this or that particular style.

This is not necessarily so. Adaptation and invention, leading to greater individuality, can sometimes be more appropriate than perfectly stylised lettering.

Lettering should be considered as part of a total design. Thus, if both a pattern and lettering are to be used on the same piece of glass it is essential to plan the design as a whole when doing the preliminary drawing. Do not engrave the pattern and just hopefully leave room somewhere for some kind of lettering which you will think about later. Putting lettering on to glass requires first of all good judgement concerning its size and position. It will be found helpful, even essential, to have some reference book on calligraphy. It is not necessary to buy anything expensive or elaborate, just one or two books which show a variety of styles.

The style of lettering to be used must be chosen to suit not only the design it may accompany, but also the shape of the glass upon which it is to be placed. For example, it will be found that a gentle, flowing style is unlikely to look as well on an austere, angular glass as it does on one with curves. It is useful to practice some calligraphy on paper as often as possible. This will help you to familiarise yourself with various styles of lettering and you will eventually find that you are writing with ease rather than copying with care. It is particularly necessary for the hand to move freely so that easy, well-formed letters come naturally and, with this, a growing sense of style and design.

Lettering needs most careful measuring. Start with a few letters, perhaps just initials, so that the preliminary measuring is kept as simple as possible. Suppose you are going to engrave three initials: having decided upon the style, size and distance apart, decide how far down from the rim you want the top of the letters to be. Using one of the methods already described, draw a horizontal line along the glass at the correct distance from the rim and rather longer than the space the three letters will occupy. Then measure their depth, and draw another line parallel to the first to fit the height of the letters. Draw or paint the letters between the lines, taking great care that upright strokes really are upright, or that sloping ones are at a uniform angle. Before starting to engrave, look very critically at the drawn letters and feel absolutely satisfied with them: when finished, they will stand alone and cannot then be altered or improved.

Having marked out the letters, take a very fine diamond with a long point so that you can see where it is on the glass, or work with a fine steel point, and very gently make the outlines. It is important to do this delicately, otherwise the outline of the letters will be cut much deeper into the glass than the filling-in, and the result will be a hard-looking edge. You can now fill in the letters by any method you choose: they can be scratched in using a diamond with imperfect cutting edges, or cross-hatched. Both these methods produce a totally filled-in, matt effect. Another possibility is to fill in with very fine lines all sloping in the same direction and individually visible.

If you want to engrave more than a very few letters in one line, you will have also to mark the glass in sections at the rim, using one of the methods already discussed. Re-make these marks on the inside rim using a pencil of a different colour from that with which the drawing will be made. By putting the distance marks inside the glass you will at least ensure that whatever else gets rubbed off in the course of work, these important marks remain.

Several lines of lettering can often appear to be crooked. This is an illusion created by the glass, no matter how carefully the measuring has been done. So when starting lettering it may be found desirable to break up the layout slightly, if the design allows, so that it is not just a series of parallel lines.

Sometimes it is necessary to put lettering round the foot of a glass or the rim of a plate. This presents special problems as the letters must be at an angle to each other, their tops nearer than their bases.

Use the marker to measure the right number of spaces round the base of the glass to allow for each letter. Now, instead of drawing two lines between which to place the letters, draw two circles. Mark the centre of the upturned base of the glass and draw lines from this centre mark to meet each mark round the rim. This will show the exact angle at which each letter must be made.

This same method is used when writing round the rim of a plate. But here there is one enormous additional difficulty. On plates engraving is usually done on the reverse side, therefore, not only must the lettering be done at an angle to fit the circular rim of the plate, but it must all be done back to front.

ENGRAVING LONG LINES

Some designs, particularly those involving architecture, require quite long lines, either drawn or stippled. Long lines always demand great care and the use of a very reliable diamond, as splintering can easily occur. If this happens, it produces a slightly blurred line and spoils the work.

For vertical lines it is best to use the wax pencil for putting the line on to the glass, keeping it as fine as possible because it is extremely difficult to thin down a painted line and at the same time to keep it straight. When you come to engrave the line your next method will depend upon your steadiness of hand. If you are able to draw a straight line without any wavering, that is, of course, the best way of all. However, if you find this too difficult you can use some narrow, *double-sided* transparent adhesive tape as a guide. (It is essential to get the kind that has an adhesive surface on one side and a paper backing on the other, not the kind which is adhesive on both sides with no backing.) The backing makes the edge of this tape fairly firm. Draw the required line, then put a piece of tape along the line and use the latter's edge as a guide for the diamond tool. The tape will help in keeping a straight line provided the tool is not pressed too hard against it so that it is dented.

This basic method is equally useful for stippling a straight line, when the tape can be used for masking purposes. In this case, however, ordinary one-sided tape may be used as gentle stippling will not penetrate it. If an effect of shadow demands that stippled light should end in an abrupt line this is an excellent way of achieving it as the stippling may be carried right up to the tape and may even stray over the edge of it. When the tape is peeled off, the stippling ends in a straight edge.

Long vertical lines on straight-sided glasses are reasonably uncomplicated as they can be drawn and measured without too much difficulty. When engraving architectural subjects it is really wise to keep to straight-sided glasses. Not only is the difficulty of measuring out of all proportion to the results, but curved glasses distort that kind of design too much to make it a satisfactory venture.

Vertical lines on glasses with inward-curving bases are far more difficult and all that can be done is to recognise this fact and measure all the more carefully (see also p. 80).

Swedish crystal goblet with diamond point line engraving, by Barbara Norman

HERALDIC DESIGNS

Heraldic work presents special problems, but it is an aspect of engraving which cannot be ignored and it can offer much interest. The designs are usually extremely complicated, being a mass of minute detail and all too often it only seems possible to find a very tiny example from which to work. There is usually some writing somewhere in the design, but the small samples one is so often given make it almost impossible to read the words, let alone to reproduce them. By the time the design has been enlarged to a scale which makes the lettering readily legible and of a size capable of being reasonably engraved, the rest of it is gigantic, with huge heraldic beasts. And what is to be done about the beasts in any case? Should they be modelled, or engraved in line? All this makes heraldry sound hopeless from the engraving point of view; however it merely presents a new set of technical problems, the solving of which is a fascinating task.

First of all, the question of size must be settled and, if possible, the shape of the glass. In this connexion I say 'if possible' because heraldic work is very likely to be a commission and you may be given the glass upon which it is to be engraved. If the design is to be confined to a small space the size of the coat of arms will be decided by the smallest legible lettering you can manage. It is to be hoped, however, that space will not be as restricted as that, and that it will be possible to plan a well-proportioned design, placed to the best advantage. The question of whether or not to model can best be worked out in the preliminary drawing. Use this drawing to plan the work down to the last detail.

Putting these intricate designs on to the glass requires great care. If you have found that you can work satisfactorily by fixing an outline inside the glass and engraving straight from it, then all that has to be done is to ensure that the drawing is properly placed and securely fixed inside the glass. However, it may be found that when the design is looked at through the glass, distortion is too great; in this case it must be drawn on to the outside surface. However, it is extremely difficult to attempt to re-draw on to the glass the accurate, scale drawing you have already made as a pattern and which has almost certainly had to be corrected many times before reaching its final state. By all means do so if you feel

Coat of arms of the Earl of Radnor, engraved by diamond point on Swedish crystal, by Claire Rome

confident of being able to reproduce it accurately, otherwise use a simple method of transferring it to the glass. Here are two that can be tried.

In the first method, the model drawing can be traced on to a piece of tracing paper, which can be pricked with a pin and then used with the powdered paint and gum arabic as already described (p. 74). This method provides only a series of guide marks and from these the complete design can be constructed, using the wax pencil. Professional engravers, however, need no more than the dotted outline.

The second method also necessitates putting the model drawing on to tracing paper, using a finely pointed coloured pencil with a hard lead. Shade over the reverse side of the tracing fairly thickly but evenly with the white wax pencil. Fix this tracing firmly to the glass, ensuring that the paper is tightly stretched. Use a very hard tracing pencil to trace over the coloured outline. When the paper is peeled off the result will be a white traced drawing on the glass.

EDGINGS

Putting a decorative edging round the rim of a glass is undoubtedly difficult. However, it is just as well to do this from time to time so that it becomes a straightforward process.

First of all, the design must be invented. This can be endlessly absorbing and a great test of one's imagination. It will be less taxing if the first excursion into edging does not involve engraving lines continuously all round the glass: so, imagine that you have invented some pleasing and appropriate design which can be repeated to the required length.

First, decide how near the rim the top of the design is to be, and then draw a line right round the glass with a wax pencil. Edgings may be placed as near the rim as necessary for the best visual effect. It simply is not practicable to try to leave half an inch clear in this case. Now measure the depth of the design and draw another line that distance below the first one. These two lines are the guides between which the edging is drawn.

Next, divide and mark the glass into quarters. This is a sufficient number of divisions for an average size glass; on anything very large, greater

Dutch crystal engraved in diamond point, by Claire Rome

accuracy will be obtained with more divisions. Try out the edging for size until it can be seen how many repeats of it will fit between the marks.

If the edging design you have invented involves continuous engraved lines round the glass, there is really no substitute for a steady hand. Measure and draw the top line as thinly as possible with a wax pencil, then simply follow the line with a diamond. It is almost impossible to engrave all round a glass without lifting the diamond from the surface; however, with great care the line can be restarted without a visible join. Next, make the lower line, and then engrave the design which is to be placed between the lines. If you are quite sure that you cannot manage to draw a long, continuous line round the glass without some help, then it will be necessary to fix up some supporting guide line. Here are two possibilities—but more can no doubt be thought of.

The first again involves the use of the double-sided adhesive tape. Mark the line round the glass, then put a piece of tape round the glass exactly on the line. The edge of the tape gives just enough support to help you engrave the line. If the sides of the glass slope at all steeply the strip of tape will have to be cut rather narrow, otherwise it will not fit round the glass at the bottom edge. When cutting the tape to a narrow width, it is sensible to mark which is its original edge as this will be absolutely straight and is the one which should be used as a guide.

Another kind of guide line can be made from a narrow strip of thin card, about the thickness of a postcard. When using strips of card, fix them into position round the glass with ordinary, single-sided tape. If you are cutting strips from a large sheet of card, use a razor blade and a steel-edged ruler to do this. Scissors will not give a straight enough line.

ALLOWING FOR DISTORTION

In original, imaginative designs the problem of dealing with the sloping sides or curves of a glass hardly arises. The design is created for that particular glass and it can be adapted as necessary.

However, in any design which cannot be altered or adapted, such as architecture or a coat of arms, an allowance for distortion will have to be made unless the sides of the glass are absolutely straight. It is surprising how much distortion there is, and how crooked a design can become, when it is traced on to a glass with sloping sides. As this distortion has to be allowed for and corrected at some stage, it is usually best to do this at the time of preparing to trace the design on to the glass, assuming that it is not to be drawn straight on to the glass instead.

Once the design has been put on to paper, it is obviously not possible to put in pleats to make the paper fit the glass; the correction must be made first in some way. One way of doing this is to cut a piece of paper large enough to overlap the rim slightly, but in other directions only just large enough to accommodate the design. Hold this against the glass and mark the line of the rim. Then draw a series of vertical lines from the rim mark. Make the model drawing on the paper, using the lines to ensure that the design is vertical at the required points. All that now need be done is to ensure that when fixing the tracing paper to the glass, the edge of the rim corresponds to the mark already made on the paper.

If it has been decided to draw or paint the design straight on to the glass instead of tracing it, it will be found helpful to mark a series of vertical lines so that the necessary corrections can be made in the drawing at all stages.

I have tried to make these explanations as simple and as explicit as possible. There are limitless possibilities of discovering more ways of achieving the effects you want and of solving small technical problems which momentarily defeat you. And, after all, in engraving it is the results which matter.

GILDING

In the past, there was a certain amount of gilding done in conjunction with engraving. This can be very attractive if applied with restraint. It is best suited to line work, where the cuts in the surface of the glass are much deeper than in stipple: the gold flows readily into the lines and lasts much longer. However, it should only be used on glass which is seldom washed. Liquid Leaf (described fully in the chapter on gold engraving under glass) is the easiest method of gilding this kind of engraving. Paint it quickly over the design where needed, then immediately take a piece of absorbent but non-fluffy material and wipe over the area where the Liquid Leaf was applied. This will remove the surplus gilt, but will not penetrate the lines on the glass, which will thus remain gilded. When the gilding is thoroughly dry, a light varnish may be applied in the same way. It is probably best to use that which is made to be used in conjunction with the Liquid Leaf.

USE OF A MAGNIFYING GLASS

In the paragraph dealing with lighting (p. 69) I mentioned the importance of being able to see your work very clearly. There is, however, often more to this than good light. Often a magnifying glass is a great benefit, particularly in the case of lettering or in work of great complexity. There are several kinds of table model available.

As this is a fairly costly piece of equipment it should be chosen very carefully—as nearly as possible under working conditions. It is helpful to have with you an engraving tool and a piece of glass so that you can test the magnifying glass to make sure that it can be adjusted in such a way that work and tool can be held a reasonable distance away from it.

For those who want something better, glasses with special optical lenses made to prescription may be used. These, however, are very expensive.

SIGNATURE

Finally, do not forget to sign your work somewhere—usually underneath the foot of the glass. It is good to have confidence in your work, and one day it may be of interest to someone to know who the engraver was.

(For details of tools and methods of work, see p. 167).

CHAPTER 5

Drill Engraving

Engraving by means of an electric drill is a method which offers considerable scope for skill and inventiveness. It is a particularly attractive form of work for those who like to see results rather more quickly than is possible by the diamond point method. I think, however, one of its greatest advantages is that it appeals so much to those who, while protesting that they cannot draw, nevertheless discover that they enjoy working with power tools. They are eager to do creative work of some kind, yet cannot take the first steps. The attraction of a power tool often overcomes this reluctance, and much interest is concentrated on the initial working out of designs rather than on drawing. Sometimes, of course, it is very evident that the real pleasure is in using machinery rather than in the art of engraving! But the important thing is that creative work is being done—and enjoyed.

Drill engraving can produce very attractive work, needing a high degree of skill, and much work sold commercially is done by this method. As we have seen, though, the pity about so many commercial engravings is that they are often rather unimaginative and repetitive.

Although engraving with an electric drill originated only with the invention of modern tools, drill engraving itself has its origins in the work done by lapidary cutters and engravers in past centuries when machinery was, of course, driven by foot or by an assistant. In its effect it resembles copper wheel engraving more closely than diamond point. The reason for this is that both drill and copper wheel methods aim to grind away the surface of the glass to produce a matt surface of varying density, while the diamond point method cuts it minutely and by this means produces its very distinctive sheen.

Drill engraving can either be used in conjunction with diamond point, or it can be used on its own. In the latter case two basic methods are possible—one more related to diamond point, the other more to copper wheel. The type of drill engraving which is more akin to diamond point is delicately done, and hardly does much more than brush the surface of the glass. No attempt is made to grind deeply into the glass, and although the surface is always matt, some of the most delicate areas can be in the style of stipple engraving.

The method which is more akin to copper wheel engraving is used whenever a deeper, more sculptured effect is needed. Sculptured designs are likely to be more satisfactory and original if it is realised that an attempt is not being made to do imitation copper wheel engraving, but that the drill is being used in its own right to achieve what is within its means.

When aiming for sculptured effects, the same principles must be applied as in copper wheel engraving. This means that the whole design is matted over without leaving unengraved areas. That part of a design which it is intended should stand out visually and appear to be nearest to you must in fact be cut deepest; that which should appear visually furthest away is barely touched and is in fact nearest to you. The main difference between working for sculptured effects with a drill and with a copper wheel is that the drill cannot cut such sharp edges as the wheel. Also, the rotation of the soft metal of the copper wheel on the glass produces a more luminous effect than the more simple matting produced by the abrasive effect of the carborundum grinding point used for much drill engraving. By combining the use of a diamond hand-tool with the drill it is possible to sharpen the edges of the engraving.

As with copper wheel engraving, it is not the deep engraving that is difficult, but the lightest matting of the glass. Having very delicately matted over what are to be the darkest areas of the engraving, the rest may be cut more deeply and strongly until the desired degree of modelling has been achieved.

Goblet with drill and diamond point engraving, by Barbara Norman

EQUIPMENT

The basic piece of machinery, an electric hand drill, is reasonable in price. It consists of a metal holder for the grinding point, the electric motor itself, and a foot control. At first, it seems a most unwieldy tool to use. The metal holder feels much too large to be able to manipulate with sufficient fluency to work with delicacy or accuracy. Its freedom of movement is further hampered by a metal covering over the electric cord for several inches. With practice, however, it becomes extremely easy to use. It is quiet in operation. At least, the machinery itself runs quietly; the degree of noise produced depends upon the type of work. No special workbench is needed, which is a great advantage to the amateur working at home. Any table, properly padded and protected, would be quite suitable as a working surface.

There are a large number of grinding points available, in many shapes and sizes—round, pointed, flat, carborundum, diamond tipped, diamond coated. They can all be bought from firms selling dental equipment. There is not the slightest doubt that for fine work on crystal, and for lettering, the diamond grinding points are by far the best. But they are extremely delicate, and should not be used until some degree of skill in using a drill has been acquired.

For work on harder glass or larger areas, carborundum grinding points are more suitable. Even the carborundum points can wear down quite quickly, so one of the first things to master is never to use the drill with more pressure than is necessary. As in copper wheel engraving, depth should be achieved by working over an area rather than by applying pressure.

When selecting grinding points, the diamond ones will, naturally, be very fine. As far as the carborundum ones are concerned, try starting work with about three points. One should be as slender and finely pointed as possible; one could be an elongated shape with a rounded end (not too large); and one could be slightly larger for working on broader areas. Once the uses of the various points have been discovered, it will be possible to build up a useful collection of different sizes.

Sherry glass, drill engraved with carborundum point, by Barbara Norman

STARTING WORK

As with diamond point engraving, it is advisable to start with some flat pieces of picture glass until the unfamiliar sensation of working with the drill has been overcome. Use carborundum points and do not put more pressure on them than is needed. Picture glass is extremely hard by comparison with crystal.

First of all, try to practice so that absolute control over the drill is achieved. It is well worth taking trouble about this in the early stages because, if properly used, the tool can produce extremely fine and delicate work. At first, the drill has a maddening tendency to run away in some quite different direction from the one desired. This is often due to a lack of firmness of touch. I do not mean force, which would result in deep, harsh lines, but only that the tool must be used decisively.

For work on glass sheets the first designs chosen can be quite simple—ideally involving as many lines as possible, as these are at first the most difficult part of drill engraving. All work should be done against a black surface, and a black rubber mat is useful as it counteracts vibration.

As there is so little distortion of a design when it is looked at through a plain sheet of glass, it may be found convenient to fix the design underneath the glass sheet and simply to work directly from it. There is one slight disadvantage to this method: the only way on which distortion can be entirely eliminated is by looking down on the design as vertically as possible, and this can become very tiring. So unless the design is an accurate, geometrical one, it may be preferable to paint it on the upper surface of the glass. If it has been decided to work from a design on paper fixed on to the underside of the glass sheet, it may be found very helpful to have made this preliminary drawing in white pencil on black paper. White paper beneath the glass would cancel out the effect of the black rubber sheet and make it difficult to see the development of the work.

If it has been decided to paint or draw the design on the upper surface of the glass, any of the methods described in Chapter Four will do. If using paint, however, it is advisable to use gum to mix it with instead of water as, while using a drill, quite a lot of one's hand is moving over the surface of the glass and it is difficult to avoid smudging the design.

Working with a drill provides an excellent opportunity to embark on much larger areas of engraving than would normally be undertaken by the diamond point method. The planning and placing of a large-scale design will pose a different range of problems from those encountered when working on the small area of a single glass.

MORE ADVANCED WORK

Having mastered the basic uses of the drill, a start can be made upon more delicate work. Very great contrasts can be obtained with the drill, but in order to achieve any delicacy of work something softer and more responsive than picture glass is necessary. As a start, any kind of soda glass will be very suitable, and this opens the way to choosing from an enormous range of glassware. The explanations given in the previous chapter about measuring the glass, placing the design and putting the design on to the glass apply equally when working with a drill.

If an engraved outline of the design is needed, this can either be done with a very fine grinding point held vertically, or with a diamond hand-tool as in diamond point engraving. When filling in the design with the drill try to make the greatest contrasts in depth of engraving. As already mentioned, it is possible to get the merest misting over of the glass as in very light stippling, but this requires great delicacy of touch. By experimenting, it will be found that many interesting effects can be obtained. For instance, a slight texturing is achieved by allowing the drill to vibrate very gently over the glass, instead of moving smoothly. The most useful all-round grinding point is, rather surprisingly, the finest one. If held vertically it will produce very fine lines. It can also be used for matting out fairly broad areas if it is held on its side. The drill can be a great help when engraving buildings. There is often a lot of filling-in to be done in such designs and this can be achieved evenly when a drill is used.

The ability to use drill engraving in conjunction with diamond point is an important one. Many engravers possess drills and use them to produce certain effects within the diamond point method. This involves working with the lightest touch because drill engraving by itself can produce quite strong effects while diamond point should be delicate. Therefore, if the two are to be used to complement each other the drill work must blend in appropriately. A slight touch of the drill over an area of stippling can be very effective in blending it into an attractive smoothness. It is also useful for the filling-in of lettering which has been outlined with a diamond. It is more difficult to do lettering solely with a drill, but at least the difficulty of a too sharp diamond point outline is avoided. It will soon be discovered that the drill combined with diamond point can be used to produce many decorative effects. Engraving by it is rather quickly done and, compared with the much slower diamond-point method, it at first gives the impression of working with a soft pencil.

Pieces of picture glass need not only be used for practice purposes. They can be very attractive in themselves and can be put to many uses. As drill engraving is fairly strong in texture, one obvious way to show a drill-engraved panel is to set it into a window, where the engraving can be seen to advantage against the light. An attractive top can also be made for a coffee table, and the engraving shows to advantage if placed over a matt dark surface. In the same way, an engraved glass panel can be made to fit on to a tray. Properly mounted, rectangular or circular glass panels make interesting and attractive table mats.

GILDING

As with other types of engraving, it is possible to gild work done with a drill. It should always be done sparingly. Two methods of gilding are possible. Treasure Gold Liquid Leaf (described in Chapter Eight) may be painted over the engraved area to be gilded. The liquid settles in the depressions made by the engraving, and the surplus remaining on the surface of the glass may quickly be wiped off with an absorbent, smooth cloth. Transfer gold leaf may also be used, following the method of application described in Chapter Eight. Both methods of gilding should be protected with a light layer of varnish. The Liquid Leaf should be painted over with Treasure Sealer, made by the same manufacturers, and the surplus should be wiped off. Transfer gold leaf should be protected by a waterproof varnish.

(*For details of tools and methods of work, see p. 167*).

CHAPTER 6

Copper Wheel Engraving

Those who want to embark upon copper wheel engraving will be following in the footsteps of craftsmen who were practicing this method of decoration in Roman times. Some of the most spectacular cutting and engraving ever seen was done during the centuries of the Roman Empire. At that time, glassmakers were classified into two categories: those who made the glass and those who did the cutting and engraving. The engravers' skill was incredible, particularly when applied to diatreta, or cage cups, in which they specialised. These were made of very thick glass which was cut away to form intricate patterns raised above the ground-down main body of the vessel. The raised decorations were then undercut so that they remained delicately attached to the vessel at as few points as possible. In the finished vessel, the main body which was once so thick had become quite thin. High relief is also practised today (see p. 107).

(see p. 107)

Another Roman engraving technique of great skill was cameo cutting, seen at its best in the Portland vase in the British Museum. To do this type of engraving or cutting, the vessel had to be made of what is known as cased glass: a vessel of one colour has a second layer of different coloured glass superimposed upon it so that it becomes a double-layered glass vessel. The engraver then cut away the top layer to expose the underneath colour. In the Portland vase this is shown to perfection: in some places the top layer of white glass has been totally cut away to expose large areas of the dark glass of the base layer; in others it has been cut down so that the base glass shows through in varying degrees of darkness to indicate shadows or folds of drapery. Such skill and beauty have never been equalled in this style of work.

Although the art of cutting and engraving is of such ancient origin, it did not again reach great heights until it was revived in Bohemia many centuries later by Caspar Lehmann. He was of German origin and was the greatest of the Czech craftsmen, having originally been a gem-cutter at the court of the Emperor Rudolf II in the early seventeenth century. The centuries during which Venetian glass had occupied such a position of fame had not helped the development of wheel engraving as such glass was too thin and brittle for the purpose. However, among several other glass-decorating techniques which were spreading through Europe from Venice, that of cutting rock crystal reached Bohemia. Caspar Lehmann practised this, and in due course adapted it to engraving on glass. This was the beginning of the enduring fame of Bohemian wheel engraved glass, of which Lehmann was the greatest master.

Lehmann first worked on glass panels and then turned to glasses and goblets. He founded a school to teach others his skills, and thus ensured that his work would continue. After his death, the political situation deteriorated to a point at which some of those who had followed in his footsteps emigrated to Nuremberg. Among them were such famous engravers as George Schwanhardt. Others including Jan Hess went to Frankfurt or, like Kaspar Schindler, to Dresden. In that way wheel engraving was brought to Germany, where it flourished equally with that of Bohemia.

APPEARANCE OF COPPER WHEEL ENGRAVING

In appearance, and intention, copper wheel engraving is entirely different from other methods of engraving. Above all, it is a three-dimensional art, and the engraver must think of his subjects as if he were a sculptor. In effect, that is what his work will be—modelling into a piece of glass, rather than onto it. Copper wheel engraving produces at the same time a matt effect and a sheen. This may sound a contradiction, yet this is what is achieved by the greatest craftsmen. The engraving is a pearly mist,

Vase, copper wheel engraved, by Peter Dreiser

yet it has a certain radiance about it. Mediocre work never seems to achieve this sheen; it stops short at the matt stage. To say that professional craftsmen have a rigorous training for at least three years may seem daunting, but not everyone is seeking to emerge as a fully fledged professional. Some amateurs are interested enough in the craft itself to want to explore its possibilities, and this is certainly possible if the price of the equipment can be afforded.

EQUIPMENT

Apart from the machinery and a selection of copper wheels—German or Czech equipment being the most readily available—space for a workbench is a necessity. This may be very small, but it must be permanent. Unlike diamond point or drill work, you cannot clear away all traces of copper wheel engraving; the workbench and equipment must always be there. Abrasive mixture, two small thick pads for the engraver to rest his elbows on, and materials for putting designs on to the glass are also needed. The basic equipment is simple, but all craftsmen build up their own increasing range of tools and gadgets as time goes by and as they find methods of work to suit them.

The most important items are the lathe and the copper wheels. The lathe is secured to a firm workbench; it is electrically driven and can be adjusted to run at different speeds by means of moving a driving belt. The most modern machinery has a speed control switch. The engraving wheels are made of copper and there is an enormous variety of size and shape available. Many engravers stamp out their own wheels, but most people pursuing engraving purely for pleasure would probably find it more convenient to buy readymade ones. Each wheel is attached by a rivet to a spindle which fits easily and quickly into a chuck, making a change of wheel a simple operation. There is a small groove in the chuck which corresponds to a shaped piece on the spindle, so ensuring an absolutely firm fit.

The more skilled the engraver, the greater the variety of his work, and therefore the larger the number of wheels of different sizes which will be used—anything from 50 to 120. The wheels are not only available in a wide range of diameters (from pin-head size up to about four inches) but they also have various types of cutting edge. The simplest are flat, like the edge of a coin, in widths varying from knife-thin to about a quarter of an inch. The other types of edge are either rounded, or shaped to a mitre. Although some wheels are made of carborundum stone, they are generally only used to achieve special effects of rather denser matting, or for matting over rather large areas. Copper wheels, being made of a soft metal, treat the glass gently and produce engraving of a more delicate texture. A modern development which is certainly here to stay is diamond-impregnated wheels. These are used in exactly the same way as copper wheels, except that the work must be done under constantly dripping water and not with oil and abrasive.

MAINTENANCE OF MACHINERY

No one who is not in sympathy with machinery will embark upon copper wheel engraving, so the need for careful maintenance of the wheels and the general care of the equipment will immediately be appreciated. The most important maintenance an engraver must do is to ensure that the wheels and spindle run true, and that the edges of the wheels are in perfect condition. Only experience, and a good eye, can show if the wheel wavers slightly or is spinning slightly at an angle.

Before a wheel is corrected, it is run at low speed, when faults can be seen more easily. If it is running out of true it must be gently but firmly tapped at the edge of the rivet; this forces the wheel back into position. (Never tap the wheel itself as this will bend it.) To test the edges of the wheels for irregularities, some engravers hold a piece of chalk against them when they are fast-rotating. This immediately shows up faults on the edges, which can be corrected with a sharp metal knife while the wheel rotates. The cutting edges are maintained by holding the knife firmly against the side of the wheel as it rotates at high speed. This literally knocks off small pieces of copper, and the job is not properly done unless this happens. Once the wheel runs true, a file can be used to shape the profile of a *thick* wheel. Over a period of time, of course, all this diminishes the size of the wheels, and they eventually have to be replaced.

H

OILING THE WHEELS

The process of copper wheel engraving involves the grinding away of the surface of the glass by means of the wheel acting on a mixture of very fine abrasive powder and oil. The oil acts both as a vehicle for the abrasive and as a coolant; it also absorbs the very fine particles of glass which accumulate. The abrasive/oil mixture should be of the consistency of single cream and to achieve this, first mix the abrasive powder with some paraffin (kerosene) then add some fine oil. When working with thin wheels, a higher proportion of oil is needed. Thick wheels need a higher proportion of paraffin. Some engravers always use colza oil, which is particularly light, but others do not attach such importance to this and use an ordinary light domestic oil. The abrasive powder is usually emery, made for optical work, and this is obtainable in several grades. As a general guide, very delicate work on lead crystal needs a fine abrasive powder (400, 500 or 600). A small leather tab or a piece of thick felt is suspended just over the rotating copper wheel, and this gives some protection from the oil which flies off the wheel during the engraving process. It also becomes thoroughly impregnated with oil and plays its part in keeping the work lubricated.

To learn what engraving effects can be achieved, and to get new ideas, it is essential to look at as much engraved glass as possible. This really means searching it out in museums or private collections if the best is to be seen. With very few exceptions, commercially engraved glass is often limited in vision. Designs tend to be worked out strictly on a time basis, and the engraver is frequently working to someone else's design. It is really a case of mass-produced craftsmanship. The engraver is certainly a skilled craftsman, but he is often using a very limited range of his skills on each design, and is repeating designs over and over again. One so often sees tiny, unidentifiable deer-like creatures alone in a huge expanse of glass, or flat unmodelled bunches of grapes. This is a pity, as vines can make a very attractive design if used imaginatively, and they have always been an appropriate and popular form of decoration for wine glasses, decanters and many other kinds of vessels. But the professional engraver, working alone to private commission, is doing wholly creative work. He will work out his design not only to meet the wishes of

Homage to the Spanish poet García Lorca. Apple-green vase cut in high relief letters and deep engraved small letters by copper wheel method. Forms first verse of the poem 'Verde que te quiero verde' and was engraved by Peter Dreiser

(*opposite*) Mayflower goblet. Copper wheel engraved in limited edition by Peter Dreiser to commemorate the 350th anniversary of the sailing of the *Mayflower*; (*above*) Goblet to commemorate the Western Australia Showjumping Championship. Copper wheel engraved by Peter Dreiser

his patron, but also to complement the glass itself; above all, he will strive for work which satisfies his own individual creative ideals. His charge may, perhaps, seem high, but the piece of work will be unique, reflecting not only great technical skill but containing within it something of the artist's mind and thoughts.

PUTTING ON THE DESIGN

Copper wheel engravers must solve the same problems of design and distortion as engravers using the other methods. The only difference is that their work is continually covered with oil. This not only obscures their vision, but means that the design must be put on the glass in some way which will not suffer from either the oil or the repeated wiping which is necessary. Each engraver, of course, has his favourite methods of doing this, but one method which works well is to draw the design first on to tracing paper. The back of the paper is then rubbed sparingly with paraffin, and a chinagraph pencil is used, also on the back of the paper, to shade completely over the area of the drawing. The oil has a softening effect on the chinagraph. The paper is then fixed to the glass with cellophane tape and the design is traced over with a sharp, hard pencil. When the paper is removed, a thin white tracing remains. In that condition it might, with care, suffice for diamond point or drill engraving, but for copper wheel engraving it must be made more permanent. This can be done by drawing over it with a pen, using a solution of white drawing ink mixed with either gum arabic or glue. When hard and dry, this will withstand the continual oil and handling which is all part of the wheel engraving method.

METHOD OF WORK

The engraving itself can only be achieved by much practice, helped by a love of the work. Peter Dreiser, whose engravings illustrate this chapter, had to spend two weeks at the start of his training doing nothing but cutting hundreds of perfect circles of different sizes all over the glass (known

Crystal vase, copper wheel engraved by Peter Dreiser, with portraits of his children on a high relief medallion

professionally as printies). In the next stage he had to group the circles together to form simple patterns. This, though, is the peak of enforced professional discipline. At the other end of the scale I have seen interesting and heartening results emerging as a result of much perseverance on the part of dedicated, self-taught amateurs. One has the lathe, the copper wheels, the abrasive mixture in a small container and the two small thick pads for the elbows to rest on; after that, it is sheer application to work, a willingness to experiment with wheels, speeds, methods and, above all, a clear sculptural vision of what the finished design is to be.

APPLYING THE GLASS TO THE WHEEL

At the start of the work, the revolving wheel is first coated with the abrasive/oil mixture by means of dipping a finger in the mixture and gently applying it to the wheel. Some engravers prefer to tip the container until the oil has drained to one side, and then to dip the wheel into the deposit that is left. The mixture must be applied frequently to the wheel so that there is always both oil and abrasive between the rotating wheel and the glass. Equally frequently, the work has to be wiped clean of all this rather messy mixture so that the engraver can see the progress of the design. As Peter Dreiser puts it, 'An engraver learns to see with his hands'. And, indeed, this is essential as most of the time the emerging engraving is obscured with a thick film of abrasive and minute particles of glass.

Lighting is an individual choice. No piece of black velvet can be put inside the glass to throw up the design more clearly, so the engraver's vision of his work depends to a very large extent on the light by which he works. Some engravers have a light shining directly down on to the work; others prefer light to come from behind it and to shine through.

In the process of engraving, the piece of glass must be applied to the revolving wheel not only firmly but flexibly. It is wrong to apply pressure in order to achieve depth of cutting, as this simply results in driving off the abrasive powder and oil mixture, and exposes the naked glass immediately to the copper wheel. The results are bad for both—harsh engraving and worn wheels: depth of cutting is achieved by working over the area, not by one hard application of the wheel. Turning curves

Whisky bottle, cut off and carved with carborundum stone then partly polished, by Peter Dreiser

is difficult to master, as a clean line at the edges must be preserved. One of the most skilful operations is that of picking up a line which has been broken off—this only comes with much practice. The glass should move against the wheel in any direction the engraver wishes.

The achievement of the right depths of engraving is one of the most difficult skills to master. In order to assess the progress of a piece of work, the engraver presses a piece of plasticine into the design. From the imprint which the engraving makes on the plasticine he can then make a better judgement of the modelling which has been achieved. The deeper the engraving, the more light it reflects.

POLISHING

In copper wheel engraving the whole surface of the design is always made matt to a greater or lesser extent. It can then, as desired, be polished to indicate highlights and show up contrasting depths of engraving. Polishing is done by means of a cork or wood (poplar) wheel and a very fine abrasive powder, usually pummice, which can be bought from a chemist. A lead wheel can also be used for polishing, but this is only applied to certain cuts, mainly very small printies.

HIGH RELIEF

Many kinds of engraving are possible. An interesting method is that of high relief, where the background is cut away leaving the subject raised above it. This, in turn, is then engraved, thus creating three levels of work. This technique is well illustrated in plate, p. 107. Needless to say, the piece of glass must be thick enough to accommodate so many layers of engraving. The same idea is illustrated by the glass made from a whisky bottle in plate, p. 113, but in this case there are only two levels of engraving.

To sum up, perhaps the working methods of the copper wheel engraver may best be described as a combination of vision, accuracy, and flexibility. He must have a clear vision of how the finished design is to look, always thinking of it as sculpture. He must be extremely accurate in achieving clear, well-cut edges. And he must work flexibly, moving the glass lightly and easily against the wheel, turning it in any direction that seems necessary. *(For details of tools and methods of work see p. 167).*

CHAPTER 7

Painting Glass

Having described techniques of engraving designs upon glass, we come to methods of decorating glass by adding to it—adding paint or enamel, gold leaf or small pieces of glass itself. Decorating such a responsive material by means of colour provides such a rewarding field of activity that it is easy to understand how means of achieving this have constantly been sought throughout the ages.

Coloured decoration may perhaps be thought of as falling into two categories—internal and external. The internal method is an integral part of the glass and always takes place at the time of manufacture. In its simplest form, it consists of colouring the glass by means of various ingredients. Glass coloured at the time of manufacture has existed since earliest times; but it was not an end in itself, it was often used as decoration both outside and inside glass vessels. Used inside the glass, it took many beautiful forms, and can be seen at its best in early Venetian glass, for example in latticinio work (see p. 22) which gives the appearance of engraving within the glass itself. Other examples are the brightly coloured millefiore decorations (very popular in paperweights) and the elaborate lace-like additions which were applied to some Venetian glass. Centuries later, colour twist stems became popular on wineglasses.

But it is the external form of decoration—painting and gilding applied after manufacture—that we will first examine. With the aid of modern materials, glass can be painted in many attractive ways. Gold and enamel

117

painting has been applied to glass from times as far back as the ancient Egyptians, and continued as a form of decoration throughout the centuries. Enamel decoration reached great heights of skill and beauty, particularly in the East, and for about 400 years, from the twelfth century onwards, Syrian enamelled glass was unsurpassed.

In Europe, the first really important step forward in glass decoration by external means after the barren centuries of the Dark Ages was the development of painting on church windows. It had been discovered that by adding silver oxide to glass a beautiful glowing yellow could be produced. This yellow glass was incorporated into multicoloured windows and was then painted with details of the subjects chosen. The painting was done in only one colour—dark brown—which was fired on to the glass to make it permanent. This method of glass painting is known as Schwarzlot (see p. 124). The greatest artists in the field of painted glass windows were the Swiss, and no visitor to Switzerland who is interested in this work should miss the important collections in museums in Geneva and Zurich, and in many churches throughout the country. Some church windows were made of clear glass, painted in the Schwarzlot method: known as grisaille, they were much appreciated in Northern Europe, and were also the forerunners of pictures on glass (see p. 128).

By the seventeenth century it had become common practice to put painted decoration on the tall German and Bohemian drinking glasses, made of Forest glass, called Humpen. Most of them were decorated in enamel colours and then fired, but a method known as 'cold enamel' was also used and in this case the paint was not fired. This may have been because much of the work came to be done by peasants who had no kilns which they could use. As already mentioned, the painted Humpen are very attractive, with lively and varied subject matter. Probably a great many more would have survived, but they were considered sturdy and were in rough everyday use.

Sometimes coloured glass was painted or gilded, or both. In England, in the eighteenth century, the very distinctive dark-blue Bristol glass was often gilded with brilliant results, and at the same period Michael Edkins was developing his characteristic paintings on the Bristol milk glass.

In addition, in the eighteenth century a very English art of painting glass pictures developed. This involved transferring the outlines of a mezzotint engraving to a glass panel, and then painting the transfer. This is not a method now used, but these Georgian glass pictures have become such valuable collectors' pieces, and are so beautiful, that a few notes on the artists' methods might be of interest.

First, a sheet of crown glass was covered with an adhesive, Venice turpentine. A mezzotint engraving was soaked in water for up to four hours, then it was carefully laid upon a cloth to absorb surplus water. Next, it was placed very carefully face down on to the adhesive surface on the glass panel. This was a difficult operation as the print was by then extremely fragile as a result of its long soaking. All creases and air bubbles then had to be smoothed out very carefully and great caution was needed in order to avoid tearing the print. When both the print and the adhesive were thoroughly dry (a lengthy process), the print was again made damp and the paper was very gently rubbed off by the artist's fingers, layer by layer. Eventually only the thinnest possible film of paper remained on the glass, and the coloured ink of the print had been transferred to the glass. The last stage was to colour this transfer guide by means of oil paints. The results were pictures of great brilliance and luminosity.

During the first half of the nineteenth century a rather endearing little decorative art flourished for a while in England—the custom of painting decorations on glass rolling pins. It has been suggested that the latter originated as containers for salt, which was then very expensive, and that they were hung in a dry place in the kitchen. Eventually it became usual to decorate them with painting, and they were popular as presents; sometimes they were filled with tea—then also very costly. The painted decorations consisted of all kinds of simple mottoes, many with nautical references, since they were just the kind of gift sailors were fond of giving before setting out on long voyages. As so often happens, these once modest little objects are now much prized by collectors.

From the foregoing, it will be seen that there is a great range of painting on glass which can be done even without firing.

COLD ENAMEL

Although most painted decoration on glass vessels has been fired to make

(*left*) Beaker and cover painted in unfired enamels. German, c 1600; (*opposite*) Cup and cover painted in unfired colours. German, c 1725

it permanent, there has always been a certain amount which has been applied in unfired colours. In spite of the simple composition of the paints, some of these very early glasses have survived—surely an encouraging sign of the worthwhileness of doing unfired painting, not a discouraging proof of its non-durability, as some people are apt to think. There are some delightful pieces in the Victoria and Albert Museum in London which have survived for several hundred years, evidence that unfired painting does last.

Many people will be interested enough to want to paint glass, but few will want to equip themselves with a kiln—unless they also intend to do other work with glass which needs firing. In any case, should not any creative activity be undertaken most of all for one's own pleasure rather than with an eye on posterity? But probably the most important factor of all in favour of unfired painting is the tremendous technical advance made in the manufacture of modern materials. Nowadays, enamel paint is made to last, both indoors and outdoors, under extreme conditions of climate, so it is rather unflattering to the manufacturers to fear that it will quickly vanish from a piece of glass which is no doubt being cherished with care. This kind of painting can, therefore, be an attractive field of work.

MATERIALS

The right paint is the first material to decide upon. Artists' oil paints may be used but, although they must be varnished, even then they are not very durable. They are best left for use on glass pictures, which will not be subject to handling or washing.

Domestic enamels are now available in small tins in a wide variety of colours. The range that will be needed will depend to a large extent upon the subjects chosen, but the number of colours can be kept to a very reasonable level. It is best to regard the paints in the same way as you would oil colours and to aim for a similar basic selection. A useful choice would be:

Red (crimson and scarlet), Cobalt, Yellow (ochre and chrome), White, Black.

These give plenty of scope for mixing. The colours themselves may not be so adaptable as those in the range of oils, so more ingenious mixing may be necessary.

The types of glass vessels which can be decorated are as varied as you wish. The only limit is to feel that, because of its shape or colour, the vessel you have chosen is worthy of the work you will put into decorating it. Expensive glass of good quality is not necessary, since you do not have to consider its texture as in the case of engraving. Coloured glass can often be very effectively decorated by cold enamelling.

The other necessary materials are few and uncomplicated. Something to mix the enamels on will be required; this can be any flat unabsorbent surface. Rags or absorbent kitchen paper will be needed to wipe the brushes, and turpentine or white spirit (much cheaper) will be needed for cleaning the brushes and the mixing surface. The brushes themselves are tremendously important. Above all, they must be very fine and have perfect points. It is sometimes possible to buy extremely fine Japanese brushes with long, thin points; these are usually mounted in bamboo handles. In general, though, the finest possible watercolour brushes may be used.

CHOICE OF SUBJECTS

The choice of subjects is endless. Some early work was extremely decorative—birds, foliage, flowers, all in beautiful clear colours, with an appealing softness. The style of painting closely resembled that of ceramic decoration. The German Humpen were of a more robust nature, often depicting coats of arms or sturdy scenes from everyday life.

If you are unsure how you want the finished painting to look, it is best to make a rough design in colour first. When working on an oil painting the need to make corrections as you go along presents no problems as you can soon scrape the paint away and then repaint. Cold enamelling on glass, however, is a nuisance to correct while working. It is messy to wipe off the glass and there is a risk of smudging other parts of the work. Too much overpainting is also a disadvantage as the more the paint is built up on the glass the more vulnerable it is to damage and wear.

METHOD

Try to manage with only a few guiding marks on the surface of the glass. Essential marks may be made very lightly with wax pencil—if possible inside the glass. If the subject has been chosen for its own sake then the main consideration will be placing it to advantage upon the glass— regarding the glass simply as a support for the painting. However, if the subject has been chosen with the object of blending with the shape and lines of the glass then the question of total design will arise. If the subject is something which must be accurately portrayed, such as a coat of arms, it is best, if possible, to fix a drawing of this inside the glass and so avoid the large amount of surface marking which would be necessary for such a design.

Apply the enamel very thinly, ensuring that it adheres effectively to the glass. Where one colour shades into another this may be applied while the first is still wet. But in all cases where one colour is to be painted over another without shading, or next to another colour, wait until the first is dry. This will enable the paint to be applied as thinly as possible. If desired, plates or other flat vessels may be painted on the underside, but in that case a plan must be worked out in advance for painting in the reverse order—ie highlights and foreground colours first.

One problem arising in this kind of glass painting is, oddly enough, one's own enthusiasm. Absorbed in the subject as it spreads ever further round the glass, you have to guard against smudging. It is very easy to roll the glass round while working and spoil the design. Ideally, only as much work should be done at a time as may easily be handled in one position. If a mistake is made, the paint may be carefully wiped away with rag or absorbent paper.

Allow the paint to dry and harden very thoroughly before handling or washing. If the paint has been applied very thinly and with a fine brush it will be very durable.

SCHWARZLOT

This graceful and elegant style of painting on glass was a direct adaptation

Schwarzlot tumbler painted in black enamel. German, late 17th century

from the thirteenth-century method of painting in dark colours on stained glass windows, and it became particularly popular in Germany in the seventeenth century when it was adapted for use on glass vessels. The paintings were done with very fine lines in dark brown, black or sepia enamel—occasionally more than one was in the same painting—and might almost be regarded as fine pen and ink drawings on glass. When the subjects were portraits, white too was used for faces and for highlights. Subject matter was very varied: landscapes, everyday scenes, coats of arms, as well as portraits and figures. The effect is extremely beautiful, and there is no feeling of restriction due to the lack of colour.

Most of the early Schwarzlot painting was in fired enamel, but modern household enamel can produce good and durable results. As with the coloured, cold enamel method, it is necessary to use an extremely fine brush; in fact, it is even more necessary, as all tendency to heaviness must be avoided. All the effects must be understated.

MATERIALS

All that is needed is small tins of black, sepia and white domestic enamel, one or two very fine brushes, some rag or absorbent kitchen paper. If white paint is used, a separate brush must be kept for it. When using dark paint it is helpful to put a piece of white material inside the glass to counteract reflection.

METHOD

Schwarzlot decoration needs more preliminary thought than might appear to be the case, as colours can be no help in achieving effects. To get the best idea of how the painting will look it is useful to make the preliminary design on paper, in dark ink applied with a brush. Use waterproof drawing ink (black or sepia) and thin it with water if necessary. The design may either be lightly and sparingly indicated on the outside of the glass, or fixed inside it.

The main problem to overcome is the avoidance of too-large areas of

Tumbler painted in sepia by Johann Schaper. German, c 1660

solid, dark colour. The dark areas must be rather understated and not shown as unbroken dark masses. Highlights may be either lightened with white, or sometimes left as unpainted glass. In fairly compact subjects such as portraits, white may play a larger part and the dark enamel may be more broadly painted.

Schwarzlot painting should always be very lightly done. The final result should be extremely delicate, in spite of the dark colours.

PICTURES ON GLASS

There have been many varieties of glass pictures. Those painted on stained glass windows were the earliest and, as we have seen, reached their full glory in Switzerland. In due course, small glass pictures evolved from painted church windows. At first these, too, were a Swiss art but by the eighteenth century they had become a very popular peasant art in Bohemia, and remained so well into the nineteenth. They were mostly paintings of religious subjects and all kinds of paints were used—watercolours, opaque colours and oils. Other kinds of glass pictures were mirror paintings which were put on the backs of mirrors after some of the silvering had been removed, and watercolour, gouache, or oil paintings put directly on to the back of glass panels. Many of these old methods of painting can be successfully used today, when modern paints and plastics make the work far less complicated.

Pictures on glass have a very individual quality. Whatever medium is used, it takes on a greater depth and brilliance than if it is applied to paper or canvas. The glass seems to give it a luminous air which is not obtained simply by glazing an ordinary picture.

WATERCOLOUR PICTURES

This is a kind of painting which was popular in the eighteenth century and is beginning to show signs of a revival. Because the paint is translucent, it may be overlaid, and there is no need to use the reverse method necessary with opaque paints.

Materials. Before applying the paint to the glass, a primer must be used; if this is not done, the paint will not adhere. One suitable primer is a new product called Nacryl, made by Winsor & Newton especially for use with all water-based colours. It has many properties, not the least being that it is a very powerful adhesive. In appearance it is a thick white paste. For use with watercolours on glass, Nacryl should be diluted with water until it is of an easily workable consistency.

Another method of priming is to use Winsor & Newton Aerosol Fixative in alternate layers with liquid gum arabic. The only other materials needed are watercolour paints in tubes. Solid cakes of paint would become coated with the mixing agent. Squirrel-hair brushes should be used and a good supply of rag or absorbent paper is essential.

Method. First, ensure that the piece of glass on which the picture is to be painted is thoroughly clean. Do not draw the picture on the surface which is to be painted as this must be kept clean and free of all marks. Instead, place the glass over a drawing done on paper, and secure this to the sheet of glass with a dab of adhesive. If using Nacryl as a primer, apply it suitably diluted with water, and sparingly. Use a large, soft brush. When wet, it will be opaque, but it will dry to near-transparency. When the priming of Nacryl is thoroughly dry, paint may be applied. It should be diluted with a solution of Nacryl and water, and each application must be completely dry before the next is applied.

Liquid gum arabic and Aerosol Fixitive are used in alternative layers because the Fixitive is necessary to provide a protective coating for the gum arabic. Fixitive may be used as the primer, but it should be applied with the aerosol spray held close to the glass so that it forms a layer of smooth liquid. When it is dry, the watercolour paint may be applied. This should be diluted with liquid gum arabic, not water. Before any further layers of paint are applied, each should be given a close spray of Fixitive.

It is important to realise that watercolour painting on glass differs from the usual technique of painting on paper. On glass, broad fluid washes cannot be applied with ease because they are difficult to control on a non-absorbent surface. The work is detailed, and the paint must be applied delicately to small areas at a time.

GOUACHE

If gouache is used instead of watercolour, the same methods may be carried out. The only difference is that as gouache is opaque it must be applied in reverse. This means that all highlights must be painted in first, and allowed to dry before the background colours are applied.

INKS

Coloured waterproof drawing inks can be used to obtain very delicate, transparent effects. They are made in a wide range of colours. When using these inks with Nacryl no water is necessary as the inks themselves supply the necessary amount of dilution.

OIL PAINTS

With oil paints, too, the reverse method of painting must be used, but a different primer should be applied. This is Japan Gold Size and it should be applied to the glass with a large, soft brush and allowed to dry very thoroughly. This can take quite a long time, at least several hours. Do not attempt to reduce the intensity of the oil paints with turpentine, as may be done on canvas; it acts as a solvent on gold size. Thinning may be done by means of gold size.

VITRINA COLOURS

A range of transparent colours especially for painting on glass—Vitrina Colours—is made by Winsor & Newton. They have great intensity in an undiluted state, but a special thinner is available and the desired strength of colour may be mixed.

    Vitrina paints dry very quickly so they must be used direct from bottles upon which tops can immediately be replaced; it is impossible to attempt to mix them on any exposed surface. For this reason, it will be found very useful—indeed essential—to have a supply of small glass jars with screw-top lids in which the thinned paints may be mixed and stored. When dry, Vitrina paints are almost indestructible.

THREE-DIMENSIONAL EFFECT

A three-dimensional effect may produce very interesting results in glass pictures, particularly as regards landscapes or still-life. In order to obtain this the pictures may be painted on separate pieces of glass. These are then mounted in a deep frame with each sheet of glass set one inch behind the other. The final glass should be backed with white.

ABSTRACT ENAMELLING

Interesting abstract effects may be obtained by very simple means for which an ordinary glass jar or vase is suitable. All that is needed is the jar or vase and a few small tins of household enamel; even just two colours can produce a very attractive result. The intention is to let the paint trickle round the inside of the jar to form patterns. However, even with such a simple idea there are a few points to observe.

One is that very much less paint is needed than you can possibly imagine. Trickle a very little of the first colour on to the bottom of the jar, and then turn the jar round until the bottom is coated. After that, let any surplus trickle at random round the sides, turning the jar so that an uneven pattern is formed. If you have been really sparing with the first amount of paint a little more will be needed, but it is best to drip small amounts of this on to the sides of the jar. If too much settles at the bottom it will take a very long time to dry. Allow this first colour to dry very thoroughly, then apply other colours in the same way, starting them on the sides of the jar, and allowing each application to dry before the next is applied.

Finally, coat the inside with one smooth application of whatever colour you choose as a lining, and wipe the rim of the jar before the paint dries.

CHAPTER 8

Gold Engraving Under Glass

Gold engraving under glass is a little-known art today, yet pictures created by this method can be extremely beautiful. It is a process by which engravings are made on gold leaf under glass, rather than engraved into the glass itself; silver leaf has also been used. Sometimes colour is added as well—as it was at the height of the Baroque period. This method of making pictures has never been widely used, yet it has persisted down the centuries and has many variations. In the eighteenth century all these came to be known by the general description of 'verre églomisé', after a French art collector named Glomy.

Gold engraving under glass has ancient origins. For several hundred years it was used by the Romans and a double-walled bowl, dating from about the first century BC, has been found in a tomb in Italy. The engraved gold decoration on the inner bowl was protected by the outer bowl, which exactly fitted over it. More examples of gold engraved glass have since been found dating from late Roman times and usually in the form of medallions with religious emblems. Then the technique, like so many others in common use, faded for several hundred years.

At the time of the Renaissance, when there was such a great creative awakening and development in Europe, this ancient and beautiful art was revived. Subjects were either religious or decorative, and the brightness of the gold leaf, combined with glowing colours, made these small pictures look like jewels. A further revival took place, mainly in Bohemia, in the early eighteenth century.

OLD METHODS

The technique, although apparently simple, in fact called for great skill. First of all, a smooth and faultless covering of gold leaf was laid on the under side of a piece of glass. Then, working with that side uppermost, very faint indications of the design or picture had to be made as a guide upon the gold leaf. Indeed, the picture could only be indicated in as simplified and delicate a way as possible since gold leaf is very fragile; nothing could actually be drawn upon it, and certainly nothing could be erased.

As the next step was to engrave the gold leaf but not the glass, no diamond or glass-cutting tool was needed. Instead, a very fine needle was used to make a delicate engraving upon the gold leaf, the needle being attached in some way to a small stick. The quality of the engraving depended not only upon the care and technical skill of the worker, but to at least an equal degree upon his quality as an artist. The work differs from other methods of hand engraving in that there was no use of stipple. Everything was done by means of lines, and the artist worked with the needle as if executing a pen and ink drawing. This meant working in the reverse way from making other engravings. Whereas in the latter all the dark areas are left unengraved, or only lightly touched, in the case of working upon gold leaf it is the dark areas which must be engraved, leaving the light areas as untouched gold.

The Renaissance artist went about this work with extreme care, realising that, to an even greater extent than in glass engraving, nothing could be rectified once a mistake had been made. Care was taken to ensure that the hand should not become cramped or tired during this accurate and demanding work, and some even went so far as to advise wearing a sling. Every graduation of tone was obtained, working right down to the glass for the darkest tone, and not quite penetrating the gold for the effect of half-tones. Dark-coloured lacquer was applied to the back of the finished work, and all was additionally protected by another layer of glass. The results were delicate and beautiful engravings—dark showing through gold.

Gradually there was an increasing interest in the use of colour and, in addition to black or other dark lacquers, engravers began to use bright colours, notably carmine and green. By means of the needle, quite bold areas of gold were engraved away, and when the coloured lacquers were painted on to the exposed glass they shone through brilliantly. The intricate patterns on these early coloured gold engravings give them considerable resemblance to medieval manuscripts. The Victoria and Albert Museum has some interesting examples of this use of colour, notably Dutch work of the seventeenth century, in which the subjects are birds with bright plumage, and entwining foliage.

Engraved gold leaf under glass and tinted in black, red and green. Dutch, 17th century

Engraving through gold and silver leaf under glass and backed with oil colour. Dutch, engraved by Zeuner in the late 18th or early 19th century, it shows a view of Sadlers Wells Theatre

Also in the Victoria and Albert Museum there is a famous and beautiful picture, probably dating from 1778 and showing the Old Sadlers Wells Theatre, which illustrates an interesting variation of this technique of gold leaf engraving. In this case both gold and silver leaf have been used, but there is no other colour than the contrasting gold and silver and the dark engraving shows through the foils (plate, p. 136).

MODERN GOLD ENGRAVING

Modern materials have made a further revival of this interesting work a much simpler matter than was formerly the case. Several methods of work are possible. In past centuries the gold leaf itself must always have been a major problem as it was so fragile to work with and so expensive. Nowadays an excellent liquid paint is available. This is a product of American origin, sold under the name of Treasure Gold Liquid Leaf. It is also available in a silver colour.

METHOD

Decide what size the picture is to be and have a piece of picture glass cut to the measurements. If a standard sketchbook size is used, for example 10 in × 7 in, it is usually possible to buy readymade frames. Ensure that the glass is clean and free from grease, then apply an even coat of Liquid Leaf. This must cover the glass smoothly and be as free from brush lines as possible; the larger and softer the brush used, the easier this will be.

If you want to use gold leaf, this involves more work and care, but of course there is the satisfaction of working with real gold. For this method, buy sheets of transfer gold leaf. These are extremely thin sheets of pure gold fixed to tissue paper which acts as a backing and makes it possible to handle the gold with greater freedom. A bottle of Japan Gold Size is also needed; this is an oil-based size, and is suitable for using on glass. It ought to be pointed out that the application of gold leaf is not immediately an easy thing to do, so some wastage must be anticipated— and some disappointment. However, if you want to obtain the very

K

special, rich effects which real gold gives, some effort is worthwhile.

The size must be painted on to the glass very thinly indeed. Brush the glass repeatedly until the size has been worked very sparingly over the whole surface. Now wait until it is tacky. It can fairly be said that it is *always* tacky—and this is where the difficulty lies for the beginner. It must be left until, when tested with a knuckle (never a fingertip), nothing at all comes away yet there is still a slight tackiness. This may take anything from half an hour to an hour or longer, being influenced by so many factors: climate, temperature, and so on.

Having decided that the size has reached the right state of tackiness, carefully place a piece of transfer gold leaf on to it, gold side down. Press gently but firmly with a cloth pad then gently peel off the backing paper. If you have waited for the size to dry to the right state of tackiness the gold will be left adhering smoothly to the glass, but if the size was not dry enough the gold will come off in patches with the paper. Do not be discouraged by some initial failure: at least the cause of the failure will be known—there is no mystery about it. If more than one piece of transfer gold is needed to cover the piece of glass, joining is not difficult. Just place each sheet with as little overlap as possible.

Another method of working involves the use of thin leaves of pure gold, which are not attached to paper in transfer form. This is delicate work as the gold is so thin and light in weight that it is disturbed by the slightest movement of air. In order to economise on the amount of gold used, and to cut down on the intricate work involved in its application, the sheet of glass to be used for the picture may first be given a coat of black household enamel. (For this type of picture, it is simpler, at least when trying the technique for the first time, to keep to black and gold.) When the paint is dry and hard, trace a drawing of the picture on it. Then, with any conveniently sharp tool, scrape the paint away from the areas to be gilded.

To apply the gold leaf, a gilder's cushion and tip are required, also a sharp gilder's knife with which to cut the gold leaf. The cushion is made of soft leather, but is fairly resilient to the touch. The tip is a wide brush made of very fine, soft badger hair. Mix about half a teaspoonful of powdered isinglass with warm water until it has dissolved, then apply a flowing coat of this to the surface which is to be gilded. Place a sheet of gold leaf on the cushion and gently blow out the creases. Rub the tip against your hair, then when the tip is lowered towards the gold it will pick up the leaf when it is about one-eighth of an inch above it. Lower the tip and gold leaf on to the wet isinglass, and the gold will flow smoothly down on to the glass. Small pieces of gold may be used for patching.

When the picture is finished and dry, apply a final protective coat of black enamel to the back of it.

If the Treasure Gold Liquid Leaf is used, the first of the many advantages resulting from modern materials will at once be seen. For instance, having applied the Liquid Leaf evenly to the entire surface of the piece of glass, it will be found that it has adhered so well and dried with such a firm surface that the picture or design can even be lightly drawn on it. Obviously only a very soft pencil must be used so that there is no danger of scratching the gilt surface. It is even possible to use a soft eraser to make corrections to the drawing. The Liquid Leaf dries quickly, so it is possible to start work fairly soon after application.

Working tools are no problem nowadays, though in former times there must have been a certain amount of difficulty in fixing a fine needle firmly into a stick. The basic method of gold engraving may be adapted to suit all subjects and tastes and there is certainly no need for it to be done with a needle, though if coarser tools are used obviously the results will be bolder. If you have been able to acquire any steel-tipped engraving tools, as mentioned in the chapter on diamond point engraving, these will be found extremely suitable. Working very lightly to scrape away a thin covering of gold leaf is unlikely to damage the fine point and will not scratch the glass.

A steel tool which is too blunt for further use in glass engraving would be excellent for working through gold leaf. Another very suitable tool is the kind of scraper used in clay modelling and by archaeologists for particularly delicate work. It must be made of metal, not wood, and must have a very fine point. Any tool that will engrave finely through gold without scratching the glass is suitable. If you want to follow the ancient method of using a needle, it is very simple nowadays to make a tool: just put a medium size sewing-machine needle into a clutch holder. The point will be as fine and sharp as you can possibly need, and the thick end of the needle is quite large enough for the holder to grip. Even the stylus used in offices for signing stencils can prove a useful tool where broad lines are needed.

When starting to engrave on the gold leaf (either liquid or pure), place the piece of glass on a black background. There is no need to hold the engraving tool vertically as in glass engraving, and the work, as already mentioned, may be done as if it were a pen and ink drawing. Tone may be varied by increasing the spacing between lines, or, as in the old method, by not quite penetrating the gold leaf. Designs should be rather on the elaborate side, as too much untouched gold will give a blank, unfinished look to the work. As a final test, hold the engraving against a light before deciding whether or not to increase the quantity of lines forming the design.

When the engraving is finished, a dark lacquer may be carefully painted over the back of it. This will show up the engraving very effectively. Before framing, the work may be protected by a second sheet of glass at the back.

USE OF COLOUR

When combining colour with engraving it is best to work this out first in a preliminary drawing. The Dutch and Milanese work of the fifteenth century and later shows that considerable portions of gold leaf were engraved away, so allowing some quite large areas of colour to be applied.

Colouring may be done in several ways. First of all, the glass-painting inks mentioned in the chapter on glass painting may be used. These are particularly suitable as they are not only bright but are translucent too, which gives a glow to the finished work. The inks may be thinned as required, and if keeping to the limited range of colours used in early works of this kind it can be an advantage to have different strengths of the same colour.

Another very successful colouring medium is artists' oil paint. If these are to be thinned, however, avoid using turpentine as this is a solvent when applied to gold size. Gold size itself may be used to thin the oil paints. Other colouring media which can be used are gouache, tempera, or watercolour. Gouache and tempera are very bright, but they are also opaque. Water colour produces delicate, translucent tints. When displaying these coloured glass pictures, those with translucent paint or inks may be backed with mirror glass, kitchen foil or with a white surface. The mirror or foil make the maximum use of any reflected light.

It is possible to create interesting effects by keeping to the small number of colours originally used. Indeed, in some instances simplified colouring may be the more appealing since gold forms a considerable decoration in itself.

GOLD AND SILVER PICTURES

Gold and silver may be used in conjunction with each other, and without any further colour, to produce engraved pictures contrasting the two foils, as in the picture of Sadlers Wells, already mentioned. Transfer silver leaf is applied by the same methods as gold leaf. If a liquid is preferred, Treasure Gold Liquid Leaf in silver colouring may be used.

If both gold and silver effects are to be used side by side, the preliminary work is a little different. A working drawing will be needed, showing not only how the engraving is to be done but also showing the areas to be covered by the two contrasting metallic effects.

Whichever method is used for the gold and silver—the transfer method or Liquid Leaf—there are two ways of placing them on the glass: either put the working drawing under the glass and use it as a guide, or draw the design on the under side of the glass with a wax pencil. Then, if using Liquid Leaf, allow the application of the first colour to dry before applying the second; slight overlapping does not matter. If transfer gold and silver leaf are used, the process is a longer one. The gold size must be painted exactly over the area to be covered by the first foil; when the process of application has been completed and this foil is fixed to the glass, inaccurate outlines may be corrected by gentle scraping away. The process is then repeated for the second foil, applying the gold size to the remaining area to be covered. Again, slight overlapping will not matter. The picture is now ready for engraving in the usual way. When the engraving has been completed, a dark lacquer may be applied.

INEXPENSIVE PICTURES

A cheaper variation of gold and coloured pictures can also be made. This involves applying the black part of the design first, removing part of it, and then applying various coloured foils.

First of all, paint a small sheet of glass thinly with Japan Black. The design is then etched through this, leaving comparatively little of the black varnish (as would be the case if it had been applied last of all behind engraved gold leaf). The exposed glass surface is then covered with whatever gold, silver or coloured foils you choose. Kitchen foil and sweet papers are useful for this. A thin layer of gold size should be put over the etched parts of the picture, and also on the foils. When the size is tacky, place the foils on the glass and smooth with a cloth pad to remove air bubbles. This method gives a decidedly bolder and more colourful effect than the more traditional methods, but it is nevertheless most attractive.

One of the great advantages of pictures done by means of the verre églomisé method is that they are best when small. This makes them particularly suitable for modern houses and flats, so few of which can easily show large works to any advantage. And, not least, these little pictures can have a most appealing beauty.

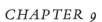

CHAPTER 9

Applying Glass to Glass

The various techniques of applying glass to glass will be described here, including mosaic work and glass collage, glass fusing and glass forming.

Mention the word 'mosaic' and to most people it immediately means a floor in a Roman house or temple, or perhaps a large-scale wall decoration in some ancient church or a contemporary building. All these associations are right, of course, but mosaics have been and still are used much more widely than that. The basic mosaic technique of fixing pieces of coloured glass to a glass base can give a remarkable effect; although few people will want to make a mosaic pavement themselves, or to take on the task of decorating a wall by that method, there are several interesting and effective ways in which small-scale glass mosaics can be used. Glass fusing, the refiring and fusing together of pieces of glass of various colours, also goes back to Roman times but has wide new use today in modern buildings, for panels or mobiles; it can perfectly well be done on a small scale at home. Glass forming, the bending of heated glass to take the shape of a mold, is a technique opening up a wide range of possibilities.

HISTORY OF MOSAICS

But before starting out, it is worthwhile seeing what has been achieved by the great artists and craftsmen of the past. The making of mosaics goes far back into history. Even as long ago as the fourth millennium BC the humble forerunner of mosaics, cone decoration, is known to have existed. This was a very simple form of work, consisting of clay cones which were set into walls so that their dyed, round bases formed a simple coloured pattern.

Mosaics, as they are now thought of, were developed in the Mediterranean area during the Greek Classical period. Their earliest use was as simple, useful, floor coverings, and by the fourth century BC they were fairly plentiful in private houses. Something hard and durable was needed for floors, so natural pebbles were an obvious choice, and there was always a plentiful supply of these available on seashores or by river banks.

Eventually, the earliest designs, which had been mainly geometrical, began to give way to much more ambitious work such as animals, human figures, fish and plants. Marble and terra cotta were included among the materials and, mixed with coloured pebbles, provided a wide range of colours. At first the pebbles had been used only in their natural state, but eventually it was realised that there was an advantage in cutting or breaking them to the required shapes and sizes. This was a great step forward and after that mosaic making became a far more controllable activity.

During the second century BC glass tesserae (as small pieces of any mosaic material are called) began to appear, which greatly extended the scope of the artist. Glass was not hard wearing of course by comparison with marble, so it was used almost entirely for wall decorations rather than on floors. Sometimes though, small, very special designs on large expanses of floor were made of glass tesserae.

After the Greeks, the Romans were the next great developers of mosaics, and their work reached its peak in Pompeii during the first century BC. They were the first to use the technique of 'reverse' laying of the tesserae, a method by which much of the work could be done in a workshop at a distance from the site. The pieces of mosaic were first stuck face down on to pieces of canvas coated with a non-permanent glue. The canvas was then transported to the site and placed upside down over wet plaster so that the tesserae were embedded in it. When the plaster had set the canvas was removed and the tesserae remained firmly fixed in the hardened plaster.

So, slowly, over many centuries, mosaics developed. The beauty and
skill of these early works is astonishing. The colours are so subtle, the
lines so harmonious, the subjects so inventive that it is hard to realise that
they have been put together slowly, piece by piece, and not created with
quick brush strokes. Much of the mosaic work of antiquity was the output
of superb craftsmen rather than the creation of artists since designs tended
to be copied many times over, and the Greeks in particular for a long
while reproduced the works of Greek painters. From the point of view
of the history of art this is fortunate as the durable mosaics are now the
only record of the long-vanished paintings.

Roman fused bowl, the pattern formed by canes of yellow, red, white and blue glass

By the fourth century AD mosaic making had extended throughout the whole Roman Empire—an enormous area bordered by Spain, Britain, Syria and North Africa—and was ripe for another development. This came with the official Roman recognition of Christianity. From the point of view of mosaics—as indeed of all art—this event produced a whole new range of subjects, religious in nature. Religious ideas were given free rein and Christian art rapidly became very prolific, no longer fearing persecution. One result of this was that most mosaics came to be used on walls rather than on floors as it was not thought suitable to walk upon pictures of the saints and other religious subjects.

Once mosaics appeared mainly on walls this opened the way to a more widespread use of more fragile materials—glass, semi-precious stones, mother of pearl. The opaque glass tesserae were, and still are, known as smalti. They are still made in Italy, and are cut from flat pieces of coloured glass. By adding various metal oxides to the molten glass at the time of manufacture, a rich range of colours was produced. Gold and silver tesserae were made by covering the smalti with gold or silver leaf, and then coating the surface with a further thin layer of clear glass. Mosaic work in churches used gold extensively. Many of the interiors were dim, and the only means of creating artificial light was by the use of candles or torches; it needs little imagination to visualise how glass mosaics, lavishly interwoven with gold and silver, must have glowed and sparkled in such conditions. The greatest of all glass mosaics are those in Ravenna, dating from the fifth century.

From that time on, the development of mosaics alternates between decline and advance. In Byzantium, where the art had reached great heights, there was a severe setback in the eighth and ninth centuries when the representation of Christ and the saints was forbidden, but the sacking of Constantinople in 1204 was the most serious blow of all. After this, however, the centre of activity moved once more to Italy, and there was a great revival of mosaics during the Renaissance. This eventually faded as oil painting was perfected. Obviously oil painting and mosaic-work are widely different in method, intention and materials, and it is understandable that after so many centuries of mosaics artists were ready to try new, more immediate techniques by which work could be executed at greater speed and colours could be created at will.

Now in the twentieth century, mosaics are enjoying another considerable revival. They are not only being used increasingly in modern architectural settings, but are being revived by amateurs on a smaller scale and in all kinds of ways.

CUT GLASS MOSAICS

This method consists, basically, of cutting each small individual piece of glass and sticking it separately to a chosen foundation. The most effective way of using this method is in making mosaic pictures.

Pictures or wall hangings assembled by means of this technique can be strikingly beautiful. There is great scope for the use of a wide variety of colours, combining them as imaginatively as possible with deliberate tiny points of light. It cannot be said that this kind of mosaic can be built up at great speed, but the work is immensely absorbing and the steady emergence of the design is greatly rewarding. These mosaics are certainly a lesson in patience because the more painstaking you are in deliberately cutting the glass into very small irregular pieces, the more beautiful and shimmering the results will be. The more numerous the pieces of glass that make up the whole, each with edges to catch or reflect light, the greater will be the texture and richness of the finished mosaic. Also, the more small pieces of glass there are, and the more irregularly they are fashioned, the greater will be the number of tiny spaces remaining unfilled. This will increase the play of light.

These mosaics can be thought of as being either pictures or designs, but whichever way you regard them it is essential first of all to see them in the mind's eye as something very simple. Some people find it difficult to reduce shapes to basic simplicity of outline, but in the case of these mosaics this must be achieved. Simplicity of colour is important too. There is certainly plenty of scope for juxtaposing colours and using them with all the ingenuity you can but, unlike in painting, colours cannot be changed by mixing. So learn to think differently about subjects. Mosaic work is so different from engraving that it can sometimes form a relaxing contrast in working methods.

Designs for engraving must be worked out in detail in advance, and carefully planned. There can be no grand, unexpected flourishes, no sudden decisions. Mosaics offer considerable latitude, and experiments can be made as the work progresses. In fact, once the subject has been decided upon and simplified down to basic shapes, you can almost let it take charge and grow in its own way—rather like writing a novel and not knowing what your characters will do next. You can try out ideas with colours before actually fixing the pieces of glass to the base.

Subjects are unlimited, needing only simplification and imaginative treatment. In this particular kind of mosaic, details cannot be attempted. Instead, a line made to curve slightly in one direction rather than in another can suggest much in the way of movement, or can convey an impression of weight or lightness. Indeed, curves are essential in any design as they maintain a fluid feeling and a sense of life. It is not at all necessary to attempt to portray colours accurately and unexpected contrasts are often very effective. The technique of the Pointilliste painters is particularly adaptable to mosaics. The Pointillistes built up their paintings by means of countless small dots of paint in primary colours, placed close together; the human eye did the mixing, seeing, for example, juxtaposed yellow and blue dots as green. This method can often be very successfully adapted to mosaics.

Mosaics lend themselves well to abstract designs, and here colour plays the main part. Of course a mosaic may be a blend of both representational and abstract. In fact, the extreme simplification of a subject can, in any case, change it nearly—or totally—into an abstract. A very satisfactory treatment of the subject, however, is to leave it both simplified but still in a recognisably representational form, and to build an abstract background round it. In fact, these small-scale mosaics are at their most effective if portraying only one main idea, and not carrying an identifiable background as well. In this way, clarity of subject will be preserved, otherwise the inevitable lack of any precise outline will blur the main subject if it is competing with background shapes.

PRELIMINARY SKETCHES

Before starting work, it is useful to work out a general plan of design.

Measure off on to a piece of white drawing paper the size of the finished mosaic. Within this limit, place the design or picture, keeping to simple flowing lines and avoiding the creation of very narrow areas of any one colour.

MATERIALS NEEDED

For this type of mosaic, the number of tools needed is small and the rest of the equipment is very simple. First requirement is a piece of picture glass for the base. A wax pencil will be needed if the design is to be drawn on the underside of the glass. All marks should, of course, be made on the underside once the glass has been cleaned. (If it is intended to work on a white or pale surface remember to buy a coloured pencil, not a white one.) A good quality glass cutter is needed of any design which you find easy to use, also small tweezers, some rag or absorbent pieces of paper, an orange stick and a matchstick. The glass tesserae and the adhesive are the most important items and must be chosen with care. The coloured glass may be bought direct from makers of church stained glass, or possibly from craft shops. Small, broken pieces will be quite suitable, and many manufacturers are willing to sell small quantities of this. The adhesive must be very strong, waterproof and heatproof and—above all— transparent. Some of the epoxy-resins are slightly opaque when they are dry and are therefore not really suitable for this particular type of translucent mosaic. A very hard, flat surface is essential as a cutting surface.

METHOD

First, ensure that all glass surfaces are clean. Once the small pieces of coloured glass for cutting have been cleaned, try to touch them as little as possible during work. Either draw the design on the underside of the glass, as already suggested, or firmly tape a paper drawing to the underside of the glass base.

The coloured glass pieces may now be cut, holding the cutter vertically.

If the cut pieces of glass are small the work will be slower, but the effect will be more striking. Do not imagine that pieces of glass, perfectly matched in size and shape, must be aimed for or achieved. It is extremely difficult to cut glass into very small pieces and to follow a precise shape and in this type of mosaic the irregularities are part of the finished effect, permitting more light to play on the picture.

When cutting a small piece of glass, say the equivalent of two-tenths of an inch (but of irregular shape), it will be found that the glass cutter can be guided right to the edge of the glass at the end of the cut, but cannot be started exactly at the edge. However, start as close to the edge as possible. Make only one cut on such a tiny surface. While it is possible to pick up the path of a cut when working on large surfaces, it is not possible to do this on small pieces. Having made the line of the cut, turn the glass over and tap it firmly but gently with the end of the cutter over the incision. This will sever the glass satisfactorily. Before starting to stick on any glass, cut several pieces of the first colour to be used: at the beginning of a mosaic, the requirement of fitting together the pieces for the desired shape does not yet arise.

It is often easier to start in the centre of a design and work outwards. This avoids the difficult situation which occurs if the work is built up towards the centre and ends in one or two small spaces to be filled, for which the correct shapes are difficult to find. Adhesive can either be applied very thinly to a reasonably-sized area of the base and pieces of glass applied to it at once, or a very small dab of adhesive can be applied to each individual piece of glass. This latter method has one great advantage: it enables various pieces of glass to be placed experimentally for shape and colour before actually being fixed to the base. The tweezers and the orange stick will be found most useful for putting tiny pieces of glass into position, the matchstick can be used to apply the adhesive. When filling in backgrounds, which occupy a larger area than the central design, somewhat larger pieces of glass can look quite effective. They can also be cut into more regular shapes and this means less work in fitting them together.

It is almost inevitable that some of the adhesive will ooze through the tiny spaces and coat the mosaic surface. This can be very carefully scraped away with a penknife once it is dry but not totally hard.

A word of warning about glass fragments. However skilfully you cut the glass pieces there will inevitably be a lot of tiny, very sharp fragments scattered about on the work-surface. These must always be kept very carefully brushed aside, otherwise cut hands will certainly result.

Most wheel cutters carry instructions that they must be kept oiled, but it is essential to ensure that no grease touches any of the glass— particularly the coloured glass while it is being cut into pieces. It is extremely difficult to clean these tiny tesserae. The glass base is easier to deal with. While working, it is inevitable that it will be extensively handled and will become soiled. However, once the adhesive has dried it is possible to wash and clean the base so that it is at least free from fingermarks each time you begin work.

When the mosaic is finished it is possible to add a few lines to it by means of a fine brush and dark enamel. If done with care, this need not look heavy, and it will produce a bolder effect.

It is also possible to build up the pattern shapes above the background, although this might really be thought of more as a glass collage than as a mosaic. This process has the effect of deepening the colour of the subject which has been built up because the added layers of glass cover the base completely and prevent the passage of any light. Thus the richer, darker colour of the subject can often form an interesting contrast to the lighter, shimmering effect of the background.

When making an abstract design it is only necessary to work out a very rough plan beforehand of the main areas of colour. Freer results will be obtained if the design develops while the work is proceeding. It is usually possible to work with larger tesserae for abstracts as no definite shapes have to be followed; the glass may, if desired, be cut into uniform rectangles or squares. This can be done by scoring a series of strips on a piece of glass, and then repeating the process in the opposite direction to create the required size of tesserae. After scoring, turn the glass sheet over and tap gently; the glass will then sever as required.

Plain, modern frames are best for this type of mosaic picture, and if the glass base is the size of a standard painter's canvas it should be possible to buy a readymade frame. Glass mosaics need as much light as possible when displayed, and this can be achieved in several ways. The picture may be hung with daylight or artificial light directly behind it. If it is to be displayed on a wall which is a very pale colour the mosaic may simply be framed and left unbacked. If added lustre is needed, a piece of mirror glass may be used as a backing. However, probably the most effective backing of all—and certainly a very cheap one—is to use ordinary aluminium kitchen foil. This gives a very brilliant effect.

SMALTI

A completely different result can be obtained by using mosaic pieces called smalti, which are made of regularly shaped *opaque* glass and are imported from Italy. They can be obtained from good craft shops or from mosaic specialists. While not expensive, it does cost a little more to use them than pieces of stained glass.

Mosaics made with smalti are totally different from those made with pieces of coloured window glass, as described in the preceding section. They are not better mosaics than the window-glass variety; which kind appeals to you is a matter of personal taste. You may like the greater regularity and rich colours of the smalti, or you may feel that the sparkle of a great number of small, individually cut pieces of glass has a greater attraction.

As we have seen, the window-glass mosaics are best laid on sheets of clear glass and are usually considerably enhanced by being mounted over mirror glass or foil or by being displayed against light. This is not the case when smalti are being used. Although smalti are small rectangles of glass of a more or less regular size and depth, their flat surfaces have slight irregularities and it is these variations which help to reflect light. Being made of almost opaque glass there is no need to mount them on a clear glass base; any flat surface may be used. If a picture is being made it is obviously desirable not to choose a base which is too heavy as by the time it is covered with mosaic it will weigh a great deal if it is to be any size at all. The cheapest base of all is hardboard. This can either be bought in large pieces and cut as required, or may be bought in standard sizes from an art shop (the latter kind will have a white surface, prepared for oil painting). If buying from an art shop do not get any other kind of painting board. Only hardboard is strong enough. Another suitable base for the smalti is plywood.

EQUIPMENT

First, the smalti. These are made in a very wide range of colours, usually in two sizes. The colours are clear and strong, and most of the pieces do not appear at first sight to resemble glass. They are usually sold by weight, the price varying according to the colour. The blue/green range is the cheapest, red and orange cost more, and gold and silver are at the top of the price scale. Usually the minimum weight sold of any one colour is 1lb. It is also possible to buy mixed 'irregular pieces', which are really 'seconds'. These are usually only obtainable in certain minimum quantities, often 7lb bags. As the price of the smalti varies according to colour it is obvious that a bag of mixed pieces will contain more blues and greens than the more expensive reds.

The difference between the best quality smalti and the mixed pieces is considerable. The best quality are a regular size and shape as far as dimension and thickness are concerned. As for their surface, this is almost smooth—not entirely so, because of the reflection of light already mentioned. The mixed pieces, on the other hand, are irregular in shape, and vary greatly in thickness.

When starting to work with smalti it is a problem to know which kind to buy. If you already have a design clearly in mind, and have been able to reduce the number of colours to a minimum it will not be too costly to buy the best smalti. Certainly the regularity of the pieces enables the work to be done with fewer problems and with greater speed. On the other hand, the mixed pieces provide an enormous variety of colours and most interesting textures, which adds greatly to the interest of the work. Admittedly their irregularity of shape and size seems rather daunting—being nothing, apparently, but sharp edges and wrong dimensions. But with a little ingenuity they can be cut to shape, and although the finished mosaic will have a less even surface than one made with the best smalti this is not necessarily a disadvantage, particularly in the case of a picture.

L

The next esssential tool is a pair of mosaic cutters. These should be the claw kind, operated by a spring. The two cutting edges do not quite meet, and this prevents the shattering of the mosaic pieces. A good adhesive is needed. There are now so many available that advice on the most suitable kind is best obtained from a supplier. In this instance, it is not necessary to have one that is transparent when dry. Two basic types are available: one which is painted over a chosen area of the base upon which the smalti is to be fixed; the other which is applied to each piece separately. The advantage of the latter is that the smalti can be placed first to judge an effect and changed if necessary before being stuck to the base. The only other, optional, requirement is grout. This is a white powder which is mixed to a workable consistency with water and is pressed into the spaces in the finished mosaic.

The same general problems arise with mosaics made with smalti as with those made from pieces of window glass. Designs should have curves, not sharp angles. Colours should be simplified. If the base is to be a piece of glass, the design may either be drawn on a piece of paper and placed under the glass, or it may be drawn straight on to the underside with a wax pencil. If paper is used, it is essential to stick it firmly to the glass base while working. In the case of a plain hardboard or plywood base, simply draw the design on to the base.

When starting to stick on the smalti, work from the centre outwards and always avoid leaving a small central space to be filled. If using mixed pieces, cut them to shape as required. As the smalti are much more regular in shape than random pieces of coloured window glass, it is necessary to work out carefully the directions they are to follow. This will show up clearly if the finished work is grouted, and clearly defined 'rivers' of grout will spoil the work.

As smalti are opaque, it is only if grout is being omitted that there is any advantage in using a clear glass sheet as a base. It is usual to fill a finished mosaic with grout, but of course you are free to create any effect you wish: if clear glass is used as a base, it may be backed with aluminium foil which will provide some extra reflection in proportion to the size of the spaces between the smalti. If grout is used, this must be pressed into the spaces, but be careful about sharp edges on the glass and if in doubt wear gloves. When the grout has been smoothed into position, wipe the surface of the mosaic with a damp sponge to remove any excess before it becomes dry.

Mosaic pictures made with smalti look well if framed very simply. Metal frames which fit flush with the surface of the mosaic are particularly suitable.

CRYSTAL GLASS MOSAIC

Perhaps the easiest of all forms of glass mosaics are those made with a modern Austrian product called Crystal Glass Mosaic. These are prepared glass stones in a wide variety of colours, made to certain fixed sizes and regular in shape and size. They are transparent and the colours are particularly clear and glowing.

The stones are made in several sizes, but unless very small-scale work is planned, the most useful size is 10× 10mm; other sizes are 5× 5mm and 2.5× 2.5mm. The colours are extremely attractive and it is a great temptation to buy far more stones than are needed. They weigh very little, which makes them suitable for use in a great many ways other than for pictures. Another advantage is that their surface is smooth so that they may safely be used to decorate objects which will be handled. The stones are sold in small packs, which makes storage a far easier matter than in the case of the heavier, bulkier smalti.

Because the stones are so regular in size and shape there is no difficulty in fitting them together. This makes them particularly easy to use for abstracts because random colour effects may be created without having to cut or shape any of the stones. Their transparency makes them most suitable for placing upon a base which will add to the effect of luminosity. The cheapest and most effective way of doing this is to use picture glass and back it with aluminium foil; mirror glass answers the same purpose, but costs more. Mosaic pictures made with these stones may also be unbacked and hung against light.

The finished work may be grouted or left untouched. If there is to be no grouting, account must be taken, when placing the stones, of how much reflection from a metallic backing is desired. Ideally, this should provide a general sheen rather than show through in large pieces.

The same general rules must be observed as in all mosaic work done with glass. The base, if it is glass, must be clean and dry, and the mosaic stones must be handled as little as possible.

TOOLS

Few are needed: a glass cutter, mosaic cutters (the claw type), a small pair of tweezers, an orange stick, a small paintbrush, and a strong transparent adhesive.

METHOD OF MAKING A PICTURE

The design, as for all mosaics, should be simplified and the lines curved or flowing. Assuming that a mosaic picture mounted on glass is to be the first piece of work, either firmly fix a paper drawing under the glass, or draw the design directly on the underside of the glass with a wax pencil. If grout is to be used, leave slightly larger spaces between the stones. Then simply stick on the stones to create the chosen design, using the paintbrush or orange stick to spread the adhesive. Some stones will have to be cut to shape, but this can be kept to a minimum if small stones are used in conjunction with larger ones. If the stones have to be cut, score them as accurately as possible with the glass cutter, turn them over and tap gently. If they do not sever easily, use the mosaic cutters. If grout is used, plan the position of the stones so that no very obvious rivers or paths of grout stand out from the design. Of course, grout may be an intentional part of the design, but this is planned beforehand.

It is possible with this type of mosaic to use a dark paint in conjunction with the stones, and there are several ways of doing this. One method is to paint simplified outlines of the design on to the glass base. When this is dry the mosaic stones may be applied over the painted design, the effect being that the dark outline shows in a slightly muted way through the translucent stones. A bolder effect may be obtained by first fixing the stones to make the design, and then painting a simplified dark outline over them. This produces a decidedly bold effect. A third way is to set a simple design in the centre of the chosen base, and then cover the whole of the rest of the base with a dark enamel so that the design stands out from this. In all these methods the enamel used need not, of course, necessarily be black; it can be any colour dark enough to make an effective contribution to the picture.

The methods so far outlined have all involved the direct laying method, but the indirect or 'reverse' method may also be used. As has already been mentioned, this was used many centuries ago by the Romans. It is much easier today, though! Specially prepared adhesive paper is now obtainable, which is transparent. This paper is placed over a drawing of the design and the stones are stuck face down on to it to create the picture. The chosen base is then coated with adhesive and the paper is inverted over the adhesive-covered base so that the stones stick to it. When the base is completely dry, the paper is gently peeled off. No special cleaning is usually necessary.

Crystal Glass Mosaic is also made with an opaque finish. As with smalti, if the opaque stones are used for pictures there is obviously no need to use glass as a base, any flat surface such as hardboard or plywood will do.

OTHER USES FOR CRYSTAL GLASS

So far, mention has only been made of using these mosaic stones for pictures, but their smooth surface makes them suitable in many other ways. They make a very attractive decoration for the tops of small tables; here it is essential to use grout so that the surface may easily be wiped clean. Although foil as a backing is most effective when it is allowed to show unobstructed between the stones, it can still add greatly to the luminous effect of the mosaic even when grout is used. So in the case of grouted table tops it is possible to give added sheen by either backing the mosaic with foil and finishing with a layer of plain picture glass to enclose the foil, or to place a piece of mirror glass beneath the mosaic.

Another very simple, yet attractive, use for translucent stones is in decorating candle holders. These are simply cylindrical glasses covered with mosaic patterns. Straight-sided glasses are excellent for this purpose—

not too narrow as the candle needs air around it. The stones may be applied to fit very closely together so that the light from the candle shines through the colour of the stones, or they may be deliberately placed a little apart so that small spaces of clear glass are exposed, the coloured stones giving the appearance of a jewelled decoration. When making these candleholders, the adhesive must be both transparent and heatproof.

Opaque glass mosaic may be used to cover a very wide range of objects, and for this kind of mosaic it is best to use grout. There is no advantage in leaving deliberate spaces for light to shine through, and the grout gives a pleasing neatness. Possibilities are: shallow dishes covered with mosaic pieces, small boxes, suitably shaped reading-lamp bases (ie curved and not with sharp angles, or with any areas which it would be difficult to cover with stuck-on pieces), and vases.

One further important use for Crystal Glass Mosaic is in fusing to pieces of glass by firing in a kiln (p. 165).

GLASS FUSING AND FORMING

The practice of taking pieces of glass of various colours, re-firing them and fusing them together, goes back as far as Roman times. The Romans valued this kind of work highly, and bowls and panels made in this way were valuable possessions. Nowadays this form of glass decoration has found a much wider use, particularly as panels forming mural and window decoration in modern buildings, or as mobiles. Some artists working in the field of fused or laminated glass specialise in mosaic panels; their work is strikingly beautiful.

Industrially, enormous projects are undertaken. With coloured glass an inch thick, stained glass windows of wall strength are made in modern designs, the glass being fused and laminated into a great variety of textures and colour combinations. It is then severed into the required shapes and sizes (which, even with such massive glass, can be very small indeed) and the pieces are set into reinforced concrete which in effect forms the grout. For work which will be exposed to less strain, this thick laminated glass is mounted in larger sections into a lighter frame (eg narrow metal strips), and is used for decorative panels or room dividers.

This kind of work, however, can be done on a small scale at home by means of an enamelling kiln. The possession of such a kiln opens up a very wide range of work and offers endless possibilities for experimenting with forms of glass decoration, but basically it may be thought of in two ways: the first, to produce mosaic panels by using a flat sheet of glass as a base and fusing pieces of coloured glass to it; the second, to heat glass over a mold so that it sags into the mold and assumes its shape—for example, a plate or bowl. Both these methods of fusing and re-forming glass may be used with a great number of variations and with many applied decorations. There is hardly any limit to the effects which can be created. Each piece of work is unique and it is impossible to reproduce any design exactly. The results are exciting and often extremely beautiful.

GLASS FUSING

Glass fusing or laminating is not such a costly method of work as may at first appear. The kiln itself is not excessively expensive considering the range of activity it offers. Many kinds of kiln are available, but some of the most suitable are electrically-operated enamelling kilns; they do not take up much room and may easily be situated in a kitchen. The kilns operate over a temperature range from 90°C (194°F) to 950°C (1742°F), which covers more than would be needed. They are equipped with temperature gauges. At the time of writing two excellent models are available. The largest of the two mentioned measures 12in × 12in × 4in and weighs approximately 40lb, which gives some idea of the space needed for this kind of work. Obviously some work surface will be needed too, but this need not be very large.

In all work involving the fusing of glass there is one very important requirement: the pieces of glass used must be compatible. The proportions of the materials from which glass is made vary so widely that it is hardly surprising to find that different kinds of glass expand and contract at different temperatures. Unless, therefore, the pieces which are to be fused together are the same kind of glass (or, to use the technical term, have the same coefficient) the work will be a failure because it will not fuse properly: tensions will be set up which will result in splits or cracks in the

Burning bush represented in fused glass by Edith Bry

Fused glass tablets by Edith Bry

glass. Much can be done to solve this problem by getting glass from the same source of supply, but in any case a test firing should always be made before the actual work of a panel is attempted.

Before planning a glass panel it is, of course, necessary to know the purpose it is to serve. Fused panels make interesting pictures in themselves, in which case they show to much greater advantage if exhibited against light, either by being hung with a good source of light behind them, or by special lighting being arranged to illuminate them. With good lighting thus permanently available, there is more scope in the use of colour combinations and these may be overlaid to create darker effects. With simple metal frames, glass panels make effective mobiles. Mosaic panels may be used as insets in windows, or they may themselves form small windows. They may also be used as permanent murals, fixed to a wall.

The finished panel consists of a sheet of glass which forms the base, upon which pieces of glass of various colours and shapes have been fused to make a pattern. The base may be clear or coloured glass; the colour effects, and the design itself, are entirely the artist's choice. The pieces to be fused to make the design may be positioned close together, or portions of the base may be left uncovered. The design may be wholly abstract, or approaching the representational. It may be found best to start with abstract patterns so that most attention and effort can be given to the firing process without too much worry about cutting pieces of glass very accurately.

Materials.   A well padded, even working surface is essential; very thick pads of newspaper will do. Other essential equipment is a sheet of glass for the base, pieces of coloured glass, a good glass cutter, surgical spirit for cleaning the glass, rubber cement, and separator (usually powdered calcium carbonate).

Method.   It may not be necessary to make a detailed advance plan of an abstract design, although some kind of sketch can be very helpful. The pieces of glass should either be cut in straight lines to form rectangles, or should be cut to curved shapes: designs involving sharp angles are not a success because, in firing, such angles do not remain sharp and it is difficult to sever a shape with sharp angles from a sheet of glass. When cutting glass for fusing, the cutter should be held vertically above the work to ensure a straight edge. If the cutter is allowed to slope, the cut edge will slope too. A margin of about half an inch should be left all round curved shapes so that they may be lifted from the main piece of glass. Either mark on to the glass the shape to be cut, or put the glass over a pattern drawn on paper, score all round the shape, then turn the glass over and tap it gently; it will sever easily from the main piece. Any rough edges should be smoothed with a carborundum stone.

The glass to be fused to the base may be held in position in a number of ways. Some artists use a tiny dab of rubber cement, some use gum tragacanth or gum arabic. Honey has even been tried. However, an adhesive known as Duco (made by Dupont) has been found to be particularly suitable.

Before putting the panel into the kiln, the shelf upon which it will rest must be coated with some substance which will prevent the molten glass sticking to it. There are several separators, as they are called, but the simplest is known as whiting (calcium carbonate). This can either be used as a dry powder and sifted over the shelf, or it can be mixed with water and painted on. In the latter case it must be allowed to dry before firing.

Artists working in this field find that quite a lot of experimenting is necessary before ideal firing times are discovered for the particular glass being used. A very rough guide is that thin glass begins to respond to heat when the temperature rises to around 677°C (1250°F). The most important point is that the raising and lowering of the temperature in the kiln must be done very slowly. The kiln must also be vented while heating, as fumes accumulate from the adhesive. To achieve this, the lid of the kiln should be propped open slightly when the temperature is around 260°C (500°F) until the fumes have dispersed. When the glass was originally made, it was cooled slowly in precisely controlled conditions, so when it is cooled for the second time in a kiln it must also be slowly cooled. This is done by leaving it in the kiln until the kiln is cold. The time needed for this will be several hours, and it is often convenient to leave the glass in overnight.

GLASS FORMING

The other very wide field of work available with the aid of a kiln is that of bending glass into molds, ie glass forming. This method is a direct descendant of the Roman murrhine bowls.

In order to do this work a selection of molds is essential. Metal ones can be bought, and these have the advantage of being extremely durable; however, many people like to make their own from terra cotta. This obviously takes time, but it does mean that there is a very wide choice of shape and design and more individuality; also that one's own favourite bowls or dishes can be used as patterns, provided they are shallow and have gently sloping sides, not vertical ones. The material, quality or colour of the original model does not matter. It is the shape and size that is important. With care, the molds can be used indefinitely.

Making the Mold.   To make the homemade molds, it is best to use a clay which is known as grogged terra cotta. The method is first to stretch broad strips of soft, damp paper or fine, damp cotton material over the inverted bowl or dish which is to be used as a pattern. Clay of workable consistency is then rolled out to a thickness of about half an inch, draped over the inverted mold, pressed firmly into place, and trimmed round the edge with a modelling tool. Make sure that the clay covering the upturned base of the mold is rolled evenly because the bowl will have to stand on this eventually. Do not worry if the visible outside surface of the clay mold is less than perfect; it is the inner surface, pressed next to the model, that matters. If a flat, narrow rim is left round the top edge of the mold the glass will bend gently to the required shape and will not fall to the bottom of the mold.

Now leave the mold to dry. When it is what potters call 'leather hard' and can support itself, turn the whole thing the right way up and neatly trim the edges with a clay-modelling tool. Remove the model, and if you want to add any texturing to the mold, now is the moment to do so, by scraping a pattern with a modelling tool. Design on the mold may also take the form of adding extra pieces of clay to form patterns. This can be done by moistening the pieces which are to be added, and simply pressing them on. A few small holes should now be made near the mold's base to prevent air bubbles forming when glass sags into the mold. When completely dry, molds must be fired before using them with glass. This thoroughly tempers them to the conditions of a kiln, and shows up any weaknesses.

Equipped with a metal or a terra cotta mold, an enormous range of work is available. Quite a lot of experimenting will be necessary, not only to discover the characteristics of the glass chosen for the work, but also to test the very wide range of effects which can be achieved in the way of decoration by using enamels, wire, metal foils, and so on.

Shaping and Decoration.   First the mold should be coated with a separator to prevent the glass shape adhering to it and a piece of glass cut to fit the top circumference. This piece of glass will sag to fit the mold when heated to the necessary temperature which will be, according to the type of glass used, around 677°C (1250°F).

The kinds of decoration which may be applied to this basic sheet of glass before molding it are very varied indeed and it is possible to obtain beautiful and original effects. For example, ceramic enamels may be used to paint on designs. The underglaze kind are best laminated between two layers of glass; the overglaze type may be used straight on to the glass as an outer decoration. Thin metal wire may be laminated between two pieces of glass—and perhaps used in conjunction with enamel decoration. Pieces of coloured glass may be placed on the glass base and fused to it, as is done with mosaic panels. Glass pieces may be crushed by rolling between layers of paper and the crushed pieces then sprinkled over the glass base to become jewelled effects. Small nuggets of coloured glass may be made by firing pieces to a sufficiently high temperature for them to contract into rounded, jewel-like shapes; they may then be used to decorate the glass base or as homemade tesserae for other types of glass mosaic work.

This kind of decorative work with glass opens the way to great individuality of design. It is impossible to copy anyone else's work— indeed it is almost impossible to repeat one's own. It is an ideal medium for anyone with a good colour sense and the ability to put a great variety of materials to imaginative use.

APPENDIX

Engraving Tools and Methods

DIAMOND POINT ENGRAVING

TYPICAL DIAMOND TOOLS
(photographs 1, 2, 3, 4, 5, 6)

SUGGESTED METHODS OF WORK

Work under whatever conditions suit you best. The only essential thing is to have a good light, properly placed. Having ensured that, whether you hold the glass in your lap, or work on a table, depends entirely upon your preference.

Whether you intend to do a line engraving or to work in stipple, or in a combination of both, the first step is to make a detailed drawing of the design. This is most effectively done by using a white chalk pencil on black paper as you can then follow exactly what is to be engraved (the light areas), and what is to be left untouched (the dark areas).
(photograph 7)

The next step for either method of engraving is to draw the design on the glass. This may either be done with an appropriate pencil, or with a fine brush and poster paint.
(photograph 8)

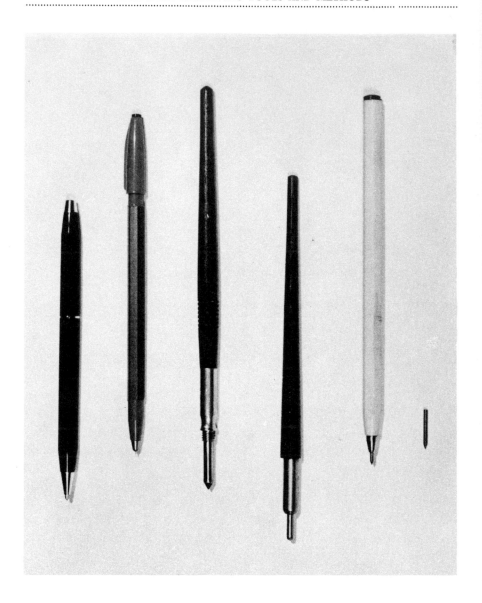

(1) *Left to right* Lunzer Lancer; chip of industrial diamond; polished and lapped diamond tip; 'writing' diamond; tungsten carbide point, mounted; tungsten carbide point for mounting in clutch holder

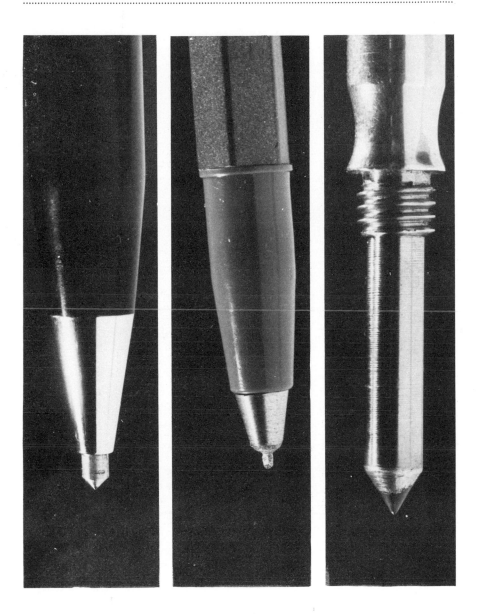

(2-4) Enlargements, *Left to right* Lunzer Lancer 90° point; chip of industrial diamond with various cutting edges; polished and lapped diamond tip which can be resharpened

M

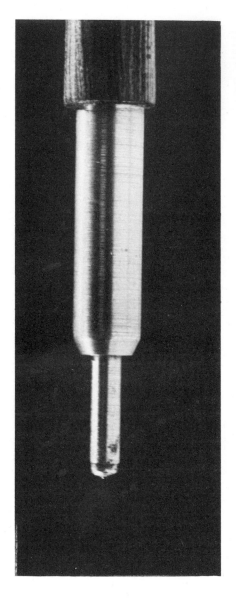 

(5-6) *Left to right* 'writing' diamond (chip of industrial diamond); mounted tungsten carbide tip

(7) Working drawing for engraving

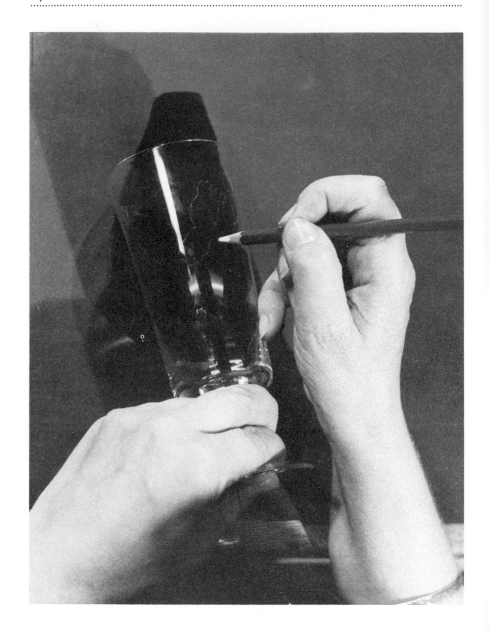

(8) Drawing the design on the glass

Next, use a fine tool and engrave the outline. Then fill in the engraving. In the example shown (the iris) this is done by stippling fine dots. (photographs 9 and 10)

If the work is to be a line engraving, the working drawing does not differ in style from that used in stipple engraving. Draw the design on the glass; outline with a fine tool and then fill in by means of fine lines of varying lengths. (photographs 11 and 12)

DRILL ENGRAVING

SOME TYPICAL TOOLS
(photographs 13, 14, 15)

SUGGESTED METHODS OF WORK

Make a black and white drawing of the design; then draw the design on the glass. (photograph 16)

The engraving is then filled in and completed by means of the drill, using whichever grinding point you choose. Diamond points make sharper marks. Hold the drill to the glass as shown in the photograph. (photograph 17)

COPPER WHEEL ENGRAVING
by Peter Dreiser

To give a step by step description of how to engrave a piece of glass I have to go back to the days when I myself was a beginner at the glass school in Rheinbach. Having practiced the craft now for so many years the technical side becomes a habit, and one does not think any more when to change the wheel, at what speed it should run or what grade of abrasive to use. It comes automatically.

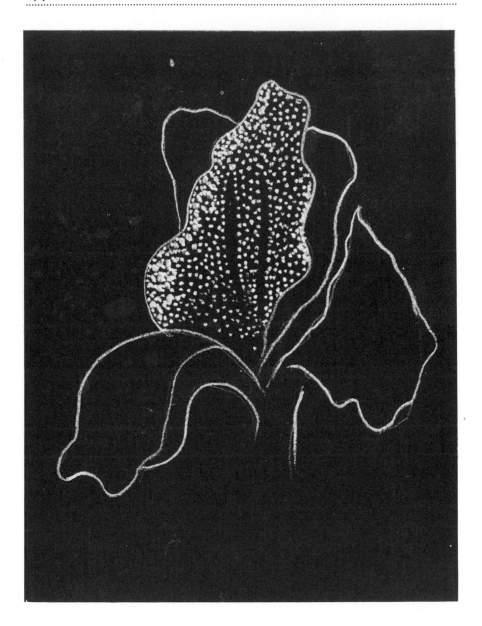

(9) Enlargement of stipple engraving

(10) Filling in the design

(11) Working drawing for line engraving

(12) Enlargement of line engraving

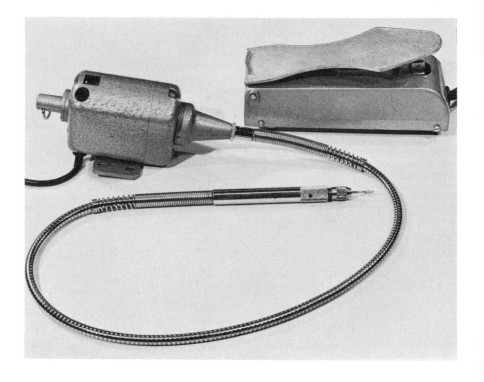

(13) An electric hand drill

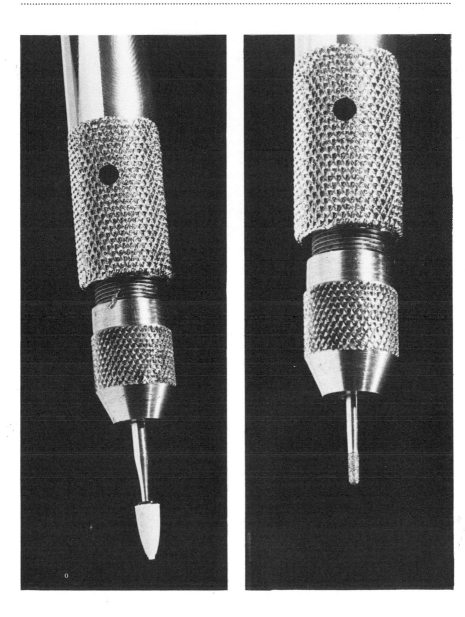

(14-15) Enlargements *Left to right* carborundum grinding point; a useful diamond-tipped grinding point

(16) *Above* Working drawing for drill engraving; (17) *below* Working with an electric drill

Technically, the quality of the glass does not matter a great deal; any glass will do but a lead crystal glass is softer to work on than, for instance, a wine bottle. Let's take an ordinary tumbler, available in many qualities, machine or hand made. Presuming you have your lathe and motor correctly mounted, let's now start on an adventure which I have never regretted.

Mix your abrasive powder (see page 106); 320 grade is a good one for general work. Leave it on the side of your bench to settle while you fix the first copper wheel. Take a middle-size spindle (when receiving your equipment you'll find the spindles will vary in thickness to take small or large wheels) and inject it with a flick of your right hand while your left hand is holding the lathe shaft for better aim, taking care not to damage the lead key on your spindle. If you find this operation too difficult, it is better for the beginner to tap the spindle-end two or three times with the pin hammer. If the key is worn away through bad injection, the spindle will never be very reliable in running true. Once the spindle is in the shaft, give it about half a dozen firm taps. This gives the lead sleeve a tight grip round the steel spindle, as very often new ones show some free play. Now engage the motor and see if the spindle runs true. If not, and nine times out of ten they don't, you have to straighten it with a bending iron which is part of the equipment.

(*Figs. 1, 2, 3, 4*)

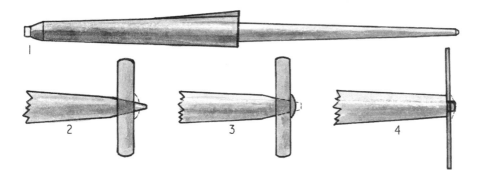

1, New spindle; 2, spindle end filed conical to take a normal size wheel; 3, the protruding part of the spindle has been hammered to a neat rivet; 4, off set spindle end for thinner wheels, to give greater stability.

The simplest cut to start with is a printy (see page 112). For this we fix a wheel of about 10 to 15mm in diameter and 4 to 5mm thick, drill a hole of 2mm in the centre and open it up a little so that it becomes slightly conical. Also file the end of the spindle conical as it rotates so that the copper wheel fits just nicely over it, showing a little of the spindle on the outer side of the wheel—enough to hammer it, under rotation, into a neat round rivet. The best way of doing this is to rest your arm on the edge of the bench and use a small pin hammer, with the force coming only from the wrist. Hold the wheel in your left hand, slide it over the end of the spindle and start riveting.

Now give the wheel the required shape as described on page 105. For printies, round off the edges; but before you start, clean the wheel by holding a piece of pumice stone against it. This will take off the burr and other unwanted bits of copper.

The next step is very important, and this is to clean the top of the work bench and your hands of all the copper shavings using a rag kept only for this purpose. If any copper debris gets between the wheel and your glass when engraving, it could give nasty scratches and chipped outlines. When preparing a wheel, keep your abrasive at a distance.

Now at last you can begin to engrave. Keep a second rag next to you which will be used constantly to clean the glass while you work. Feed the wheel (see page 112), having both elbows firmly embedded in the pads (filled with bran); bring the glass up to the lower part of the wheel and apply gentle pressure. Don't move the tumbler in any direction, just keep it still, using your thumbs to clean away the oil and see what you have cut. To your amazement you will see a small indentation. Up to now it was easy. The tricky part is to enlarge the dot into a round printy. The answer is just practice. If you give up at this stage do not bother to try something else hoping it will be easier. In wheel engraving nothing comes easily. Even after twenty years I still have my anxious moments, so don't worry if your printies for a few days look more like Spanish tomatoes. It will come with perseverance. Once the printy has been mastered, proceed by grouping them into four, five or six, just touching each other.

By now you must have noticed that when moving the glass slowly along the wheel, it is possible to cut different shapes, and as you become more experienced you will require wheels of different thicknesses, and profiles. Thinner wheels need an off-set rivet to give them more stability, as seen in *fig. 4.* Try keeping to shapes derived from printies and olives. The seal engravers of ancient Mesopotamia used mainly these two shapes to great advantage. Some of them are very crude if compared with Roman standards, but here one can see how, out of just two simple cuts and a few simple lines, they composed flowers, animals and even the human figure. The British Museum displays a fine collection of these seals.

(*Figs. 5, 6, 7, 8, 9, 10*)

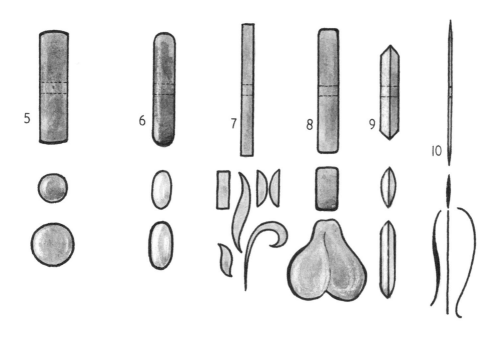

5, Profile of wheel to cut printies; 6,. profile of wheel to cut olives; 7, strap wheel, using it straight and also the inner and outer edge; 8, for cutting out defined shapes as in figure work; 9, mitre cut not often used in copper wheel engraving but the most used wheel in glass cutting; 10, wheel used for thick or thin lines can, if desired, be turned down to a razor edge.

11, Simple combinations of the various cuts for the beginner.

At a later stage when cutting out more defined shapes you will find it best to use a strap wheel with both its sharp edges rounded off (see *fig. 8*). It will give you a greater working surface. The advantage of using this type of wheel is that you obtain a shallow engraving without losing any sculptural effect, while a more rounded wheel will give a deeper engraving which looks clumsy and heavy. This is best observed by comparing engraved glass of the seventeenth century with that of the eighteenth and early nineteenth centuries. Finally, when the whole work has been completed, bring it to life by polishing gently a few highlights here and there with a cork wheel. Here a word of caution: when using a cork wheel, polish very carefully and only small areas at a time. Then clean the glass and dry it, in order to examine the extent and effect of the polishing. The beginner is always inclined to over-polish, which makes the engraving look very oily; it is better to keep it slightly under-polished. The only way to correct too much polishing is by matting the design all over again.

In this short summary of copper wheel engraving for the beginner I have tried to give an accurate picture of how it is done. There is no mystery; just practice and determination.

There are a number of other abrasive wheels, some impregnated with diamond, and also the synthetic stones. All have their uses and, successfully combined, can give very interesting results as you can see from the illustrations here reproduced. But copper wheel engraving on its own is supreme, and—to my mind—will surpass all other forms of decorating glass. It is therefore a great pity that this craft is so neglected in the colleges and art schools, for no matter how many books are written on the subject they will never be a replacement for a good teacher. To learn this artistic craft well, working with one of the most beautiful man-made materials, so ancient and yet indispensable to the modern world, the guidance of an experienced craftsman is an unrivalled aid.

N

Glossary

Carborundum	A hard abrasive (compound of carbon and silicon).
Cold enamel	Painted decoration in unfired colours.
Enamel	Painted decoration in colours which are fired.
Fuse	To join together by melting.
Gouache	Opaque water colours. (Sold in tubes or jars.)
Grog	Ground up pieces of previously fired ceramic material, mixed with fresh unfired clay to give thicker consistency and reduce shrinkage.
Laminate	To overlay in layers.
Mezzotint	An engraving which concentrates on tone rather than line. It is first made on a copper plate with special metal tools, ink is applied to the plate, and a print made on paper.
Paint	In this book the word is used as a general description of applied colours. Individual techniques are specified where necessary.
Tempera	Opaque paint, mixed with a special emulsion. Both paint and emulsion are available at art shops.

Addresses where materials may be obtained

The following is a list of firms known to me, but
there are many more who could supply materials.

SUPPLIERS IN ENGLAND

DIAMOND ENGRAVING TOOLS
Dubbeldee Diamond Co Ltd,
Audrey House,
Ely Place,
London, EC1.

Shaw Abrasives (Diamond) Ltd,
Waterloo Road,
London, NW2 7UN.

L. M. van Moppes & Sons Ltd,
Basingstoke,
Hants.

Agents for Lunzer Lancer:
Comb Binding Ltd,
124-6 Montague Street,
Worthing,
Sussex.

TUNGSTEN CARBIDE ENGRAVING TOOLS
Production Tool Alloy Co Ltd,
Sharpenhoe,
Bedford.
(For tips mounted in holders)

Messrs Wickman,
PO Box 44,
Coventry.
(For tips only. H. Grade Wimet bar)
$\frac{1}{16} \times \frac{5}{8}$)

ELECTRIC HAND DRILLS
A. II. Ritchie & Co,
24 Southwark Street,
London, SE1.

CRYSTAL GLASS MOSAIC
Enamelaire Ltd,
61b High Street,
Watford,
Herts.

ELECTRIC KILNS
Enamelaire Ltd,
61b High Street,
Watford,
Herts.

SUPPLIERS IN THE USA

DIAMOND ENGRAVING TOOLS
  Lunzer Industrial Diamonds Inc,
  48 West 48th Street,
  New York, NY, 10036.

CRYSTAL GLASS MOSAIC
  Wepra Co,
  49 West 37th Street,
  New York, NY, 10018.

  L. Levin Co,
  100 Fountain Street,
  Providence, RI.

NACRYL
  Information from:
  Winsor & Newton Inc,
  555 Winsor Drive,
  Secaucus,
  NJ 07094.

Books for Further Reading

GENERAL READING

DAVIS, Derek C. and MIDDLEMISS, Keith. *Coloured Glass* (1968)

DAVIS, Frank. *The Collector's Week-End Book* (1956)

ELVILLE, E. M. *The Collector's Dictionary of Glass* (1961)

GROS-GALLINER, Gabriella. *Glass* (1970)

HARDEN, D. B., PAINTER, K. S., PINDER-WILSON, R. H., TAIT, Hugh. *Masterpieces of Glass* (British Museum 1968)

HONEY, W. B. *English Glass* (1946)

HUGHES, G. Bernard. *English Glass for the Collector* (1958)

HUGHES, G. Bernard. *Country Life Collectors' Book* (1963)

HUNTER, Frederick William. *Stiegel Glass* (New York 1950)

KÄMPFER and BEYER. *Glass* (1966), originally *4000 Jahre Glas* (Dresden 1966)

PLANT, James S. *Steuben Glass* (New York 1951)

SAVAGE, George. *Glass* (1965)

WILKINSON, O. N. *Old Glass* (1968)

DIAMOND POINT ENGRAVING

BUCKLEY, Wilfred. *Diamond Engraved Glass of the 16th Century* (1929)
BUCKLEY, Wilfred. *Frans Greenwood and the Glasses that He Engraved* (1930)
BUCKLEY, Wilfred. *Aert Schouman and the Glasses that He Engraved* (1931)
BUCKLEY, Wilfred. *D. Wolff and the Glasses that He Engraved* (1935)
WHISTLER, Laurence. *Engraved Glass 1952-1958* (1959)

GLASS PAINTING

CLARKE, H. G. *The Story of Old English Glass Pictures* (1928)
VYDRA, Josef. *Folk Painting on Glass* (1957)

GOLD ENGRAVING UNDER GLASS

EDEN, F. Sydney. 'Verre Eglomisé', *The Connoisseur Magazine* (1932)
HONEY, W. B. 'Gold Engraving Under Glass', *The Connoisseur Magazine* (1933)

MOSAICS

GARNETT, Angelica. *Mosaics* (1967)
HENDRIKSON, Edwin A. *Mosaics: Hobby and Art* (New York 1957)
HUTTON, Helen. *Mosaic Making* (New York and London 1966)
JENKINS, Louisa and MILLS, Barbara. *The Art of Making Mosaics* (Princeton, New Jersey 1957)
KINNEY, Kay. *Glass Craft* (London, Philadelphia and Toronto 1962)
LUCHNER, Adolf. *Crystal Glass Mosaic* (1969), originally *Leuchtendes Kristall-glas* (Stuttgart)
STRIBLING, Mary Lou. *Mosaic Techniques* (1966)
TANNER, June. *Let's Make a Mosaic* (Sydney 1968)
UNGER, Hans. *Practical Mosaics* (1965)
WOOD, Paul W. *Stained Glass Crafting* (New York 1967: London and Sydney 1968)
YOUNG, Joseph L. *Mosaics* (New York 1957)

Acknowledgments

I should like to record my thanks to the many people who have so willingly given me help while writing this book. I am particularly grateful to Desmond Hawkins who has written the foreword, and without whose help the book would never have been undertaken.

Mrs Claire Rome provided information about diamond tools and gave photographs of her own diamond point engraving. Mrs Edith Bry, of New York City, supplied helpful advice in connection with fused glass, and gave photographs of her work. Peter Dreiser was unsparing of his time and knowledge on the subject of copper wheel engraving, and his own photographs illustrate that chapter. Roy Youngs, Senior Technical Instructor, Department of Light Transmission & Projection at the Royal College of Art, supplied technical information. Mr W. Leask of Sidmouth gave useful information on his method of making pictures with gold leaf and black enamel.

I am grateful to the Glass Manufacturers' Federation for the use of their library, and for the help given by the Federation's Librarian, Miss Lewis. The Research Staff at Bourne Hall Library, Ewell, also supplied valuable material.

Finally, my thanks are due to John Green who helped with the illustrations and took the photographs of my own work.

Index